The 7 Secrets to *Essential Speaking*

FIND YOUR VOICE
CHANGE YOUR LIFE

Doreen Downing, PhD

Copyright © 2022 Doreen Downing, PhD

Cover art copyright © 2022 Tim Ford

The 7 Secrets to Essential Speaking: Find Your Voice, Change Your Life: by Doreen Downing, PhD. Copyright © 2022 Doreen Downing, PhD.

All rights reserved. No part of this book may be reproduced or transmitted in any form by any means, electronic or mechanical, including photocopying, recording, or by any information storage and retrieval system, without written permission from the author, except for the inclusion of a brief quotation in a review.

The material in this book is intended for educational purposes only. No expressed or implied guarantee as to the effects of the use of the recommendation can be given nor liability taken.

ISBN: 978-1-7379745-0-5

Library of Congress Control Number: 2022901685

Larkspur Publishing
154 Larkspur Plaza Drive
Larkspur, CA 94939

Scan this code to access Doreen Downing's website:

What Clients Say About Coaching with Doreen Downing, PhD

"I walked away from coaching with Doreen not only with new confidence and a solid framework in which to approach public speaking, but also with a deeper understanding of the power of presence."

~ Denise Rose, Life Coach

"This is not your typical coaching on public speaking. It digs deep into your being and helps you be comfortable. It is life-changing!"

~ Cynthia Torres, Compliance Officer

"My work with Doreen has helped me find my way to my core self and to access my inner strength faster than I may have been able to do on my own. I can stay grounded, focused, and connected in a time of great upheaval."

~ Stephen Danner, Development Director

"I overcame an obstacle from my past that caused anxiety about public speaking. One of the secrets is BEING PRESENT in the here and now, not returning back to that experience every time I have to speak publicly. I now have tools to redirect my brain to overcome the negative aspects of that past experience and can look at the positive."

~ Dale Scoggin, VP Sales

"I now have more confidence speaking in groups and with individuals. I learned that I can have fear and also embrace my fear as my friend. All the techniques I have learned from Doreen have taught me how to refocus and be comfortable with myself."

~ Barbara Crump, Nurse

"My seminar went incredibly well. I had rave reviews. I was impactful, and I even had people tell me that I'm a natural at public speaking. I owe it ALLLL to Doreen."

~ Summer Maher, Sales

"Doreen has helped me to expand and evolve in ways I didn't think were possible. Forever grateful!"

~ Tessa Groener, Volunteer

"As a result of working with Doreen, I was able to have public speaking experiences that went from slight nervousness in the beginning of coaching to complete confidence and even excitement and joy while speaking."
~ Mira Bieler, Program Producer

"In just one session, Doreen gave me valuable skills for presenting and leading meetings."
~ Niki Mott, Teacher and Facilitator

"I went on a journey of self-discovery where I learned what my true essence was and how to let it shine through as I speak. I truly learned to value and appreciate the present moment and how valuable that is when speaking."
~ Hashi Richards, Attorney

"Working with Doreen was truly transformational."
~ John Basile, Associate Director

"Doreen has given me tools to take with me into my everyday life. I have deepened my ability to express and to share myself with authenticity."
~ Angela Ocone, Spiritual Teacher

"I received lifelong tools for engaging with everyone in my life, not just [for] public speaking."
~ Claire Wood, Administrator

"I found an inner, grounded, real sense of confidence in my everyday personal life and work life. I found my voice and my strength, which was awaiting inside of me."
~ Sarah Malik, Coach

"I've learned where my fear of speaking comes from. I found my place of inner stillness and peace, and now speak with confidence. I use these tools nearly every day in conversations, presentations, and meetings."
~ Matthew Price, Accountant

"Doreen's coaching sessions helped me to reach the source of my anxiety around speaking. More importantly, what I learned has helped me to reconnect with my true self, and I feel the benefits of that every day."
~ Cara Moutsos, Health Practitioner

Table of Contents

AUTHOR'S NOTE	9
PREFACE	11
The Foundations of Essential Speaking	12
The Power of Essential Speaking	13
Change Begins Now	14
INTRODUCTION	17
How to Use This Book	23
CHAPTER 1: FEAR OF PUBLIC SPEAKING	27
How Fear Shows Up	29
How Does Fear Show Up in Your Body?	31
Is Your Fear Stronger Before, During, or After a Talk?	32
Are You More Afraid of Familiar or Unfamiliar Groups?	33
Are You Afraid to Be Seen?	34
Avoid the Fear or Mask It	34
Do You Avoid the Fear?	35
Do You Mask the Fear?	36
What Causes the Fear?	37
Childhood	38
Family	38
Personality	39
Teachers	40
Peers	41
Work	41
Culture	42
Summary	43
Exercise: Facing Your Fear of Public Speaking	44
CHAPTER 2: FEAR OF BEING REAL IN PUBLIC	47
Fear of Being Your True Self	49
My Journey into the Real Fear	52
Toastmasters	52

Acting Classes	53
Speaking Circles	55
Facing the Fear of Being Real	56
Summary	59
Exercise: Facing Your Fear of Being Real in Public	60

CHAPTER 3: THE 7 SECRETS TO ESSENTIAL SPEAKING — 61

- Secret 1 — BE Silent — 66
- Secret 2 — BE Present — 71
- Secret 3 — BE Aware — 76
- Secret 4 — BE Attuned — 83
- Secret 5 — BE Positive — 89
- Secret 6 — BE Connected — 95
- Secret 7 — BE Yourself — 99
- Summary — 105

CHAPTER 4: MASTERING THE 7 SECRETS TO ESSENTIAL SPEAKING — 107

- Options for Finding Your Voice—with Help — 109
  - *Working with Me* — 109
  - *Speaking Circles* — 111
  - *Practicing on Your Own* — 111
  - *Practicing in a Group* — 112
- Summary — 113

CHAPTER 5: GUIDELINES FOR A PRACTICE GROUP — 115

- Purpose of the Group — 115
- Setting up the Group — 116
- Agreements for the Group — 117
- Instructions for a Practice Group — 117
- Exercises for Practicing Each Secret — 118
  - *Secret 1 — BE Silent* — 118
  - *Secret 2 — BE Present* — 120
  - *Secret 3 — BE Aware* — 123
  - *Secret 4 — BE Attuned* — 125
  - *Secret 5 — BE Positive* — 128
  - *Secret 6 — BE Connected* — 130
  - *Secret 7 — BE Yourself* — 132

From Practice to Mastery	133
Connection	134
Engagement	135
Summary	135
CHAPTER 6: ESSENTIAL SPEAKING IN DAILY LIFE	137
Essential Speaking to Yourself	137
Essential Speaking with Family	140
Essential Speaking at Work	145
Essential Speaking for World Peace	149
Summary	154
ACKNOWLEDGMENTS	155
INDEX	157
ABOUT THE AUTHOR	161
WHERE TO FIND PROGRAMS WITH DOREEN DOWNING, PHD	163

Author's Note

Shortly after publication of this book in 2009, I got married! Now, twelve years later as I'm updating the book, I'm also updating my name for this edition.

I realized that while the former title—*Essential Speaking: The 7-Step Guide to Finding Your Real Voice*—still reflects my work, it does not fully embody the meaning and scope of the process I now teach to my coaching clients. And I wanted my book to address this.

Since "Essential Speaking" is about finding your true voice, I am republishing the book under the title: *The 7 Secrets to Essential Speaking: Find Your Voice, Change Your Life.*

Why the title change? Because I felt the need to come up with one that more closely resonates with what I know people are truly looking for, from my years of helping so many transform their fear of public speaking: to find their voice and change their life.

However, this book will still center around Essential Speaking. Because finding your true voice is about finding your true Essence and speaking directly from that Essence.

I've changed the "7 Steps" to "7 Secrets," because I believe "Secrets" conveys more clearly what the journey to your authentic Self entails. The path to find your true Essence is an inner one, where you discover more of who you truly are. When you reach the Essence of who you are, your speaking flows easily and effortlessly.

Author's Note

Another reason I've shifted to using "Secrets" is because I believe the term itself requires people to pause, to consider, to ask themselves "How?" and "Why?" rather than to merely take a step. A step is something to be taken or not taken; a *secret*, on the other hand, is something to discover, to understand, and to internalize before taking the action that will make it yours forever.

May the 7 Secrets in this book encourage you to reach the Essence of who you really are, and to cherish the experience of speaking from there.

Preface

In early 2000, I opened a catalog of courses being offered at the Learning Annex in San Francisco and my eye caught the title of a new program: "7 Steps to Fearless Speaking." I was stunned. For eight years, I had been teaching a monthly class at the Annex titled "How to Overcome Your Fear of Public Speaking." Since my students typically raved about the breakthroughs and transformation they experienced as a direct result of this one-evening class, I wondered why another instructor had been hired to conduct a program so similar to mine.

But then, reading further, I saw that I was listed as the teacher of the new course. I called the director of the Learning Annex to discuss the misprint. She informed me that the suggested title change had been sent for my approval; they assumed that I had responded in the affirmative. I had never received such a notice.

As happens in many cases, this challenge turned out to be a disguised opportunity. Since I had been delivering the material successfully for many years, it was a simple process to create the new curriculum. I reorganized the course content into the promised seven steps, and in the process discovered a format that has since helped thousands of people overcome stage fright, learn to be themselves in public, and speak with confidence in front of others. These steps served as the foundation of the first edition of this book. They have since been upgraded to "7 Secrets." (See "Author's Note" for the reasons and benefits underlying this change.)

The Foundations of Essential Speaking

As I will soon relate, I once suffered terrible anxiety when called upon to speak in public—so much so that I avoided the experience at all costs.

This dread is not uncommon. Having to give a presentation, manage a meeting, or report to colleagues is a leading cause of anxiety in our society, and it inhibits men and women from living fully in numerous aspects of their lives, even if they seldom have opportunities for public speaking.

I wrote the first edition of this book—*Essential Speaking: The 7-Step Guide to Finding Your Real Voice*—to show how the fear of speaking in public could be dissolved in a systematic and natural way. And the feedback I received told me that this was really working for those who used this process.

Now, in this second edition—*The 7 Secrets to Essential Speaking: Find Your Voice, Change Your Life*—the process of discovering and claiming your voice is much the same as in the first edition, except that I reveal secrets instead of steps so that you can consult your innermost Self to help you unfold your speaking capacities rather than just follow given steps.

This powerful process goes beyond merely relieving your nervousness or helping you control the butterflies in your stomach. The Secrets I offer lead to a deep and abiding solution, releasing you from the terror you encounter when a group focuses its attention on you and the shame you suffer afterwards because you believed you were not good enough. These Secrets help create change in your very Essence so that you are liberated from old patterns, become centered in your Self, and are happy to speak at every opportunity to do so.

In this book, you will find writing exercises designed to help you understand and eliminate your fear. Use a journal to note your discoveries. Instructions for exploring each Secret and suggestions for forming a support group are supplied. Integrating the Secrets in this book will gradually free you from anxiety and build your self-confidence, one step at a time.

My intention is to help you understand that your authentic power lies in who you are—your *natural presence*. When you speak from this place, your voice is supported by the strength of your convictions and genuine self-knowledge.

In learning to connect to your Essence, you will tap into your natural strength and find the confidence to express what you really have to say, whether in front of an audience, at work, or with your loved ones.

The Power of Essential Speaking

The conventional approach to overcoming the fear of public speaking offers suggestions about what to wear and how to craft words, develop humor, and express emphasis with gestures or dramatic pauses. It is based on the notion that speaking in front of people is like a stage performance. It assumes that you need a script, and that your goal is to be entertaining. The focus is on perfecting your act, rather than sharing who you essentially are. These approaches view audience members as evaluators, ready to criticize what you have to say.

The problem with the conventional approach is that it is superficial, and that it covers over your fear and tension. When the real issues are not addressed, the underlying shaky foundation persists. To heal your deep anxieties and become a truly powerful presenter of information and ideas, you need a different approach.

The program I present in this book is not about rendering a speech, selecting the right outfit, or dramatizing for effect. Nor is it about preparation that involves breathing deeply, visualizing, or rehearsing. Of course, what you say does need to be arranged so that others can understand it, and being prepared is appropriate. But the cleverest script doesn't help when you miss a line, get lost in the middle of what you are saying, or go absolutely blank.

What will you do if your nervousness knocks all the words out of your mind? A good joke may put the audience at ease, but if they don't laugh at it, will you be comfortable enough to continue on course? Being theatrical to highlight a point or make an impression can be a useful technique. Your real goal, however, is to give your audience a lasting impression of yourself as a person who is genuine, sincere, and compelling.

Change Begins Now

Many people, when faced with a speaking engagement they can't circumvent, make up excuses, over-prepare, and try desperately to mask the discomfort they feel. They defer to others, or cut themselves short by saying a bare minimum of words.

But the fear doesn't disappear. It goes underground, remains hidden, and over time deepens and becomes more insidious. The risk of exposing one's anguish increases, and with it grows apprehension regarding the fear itself. The anxiety about speaking is compounded by the terror that it will be unmasked. And so the wondrous human potential buried within people who feel constrained in this way remains tragically untapped—until true change is set in motion.

This book is for people who feel anxious about speaking in front of groups and want to know why they feel this way and what they can do to change. Whether you are nervous about expressing yourself in a group or feel shy about conversing privately with just one other person, these pages will show you a way to increase your resolution and your willingness to say what you really mean, regardless of the circumstances. You will take the steps necessary to move forward through your fear so that you can transform yourself and your life. You will be able to speak up and speak out in places and ways you never before thought possible.

My clients tell me that the Essential Speaking process works for them; and it can work for you, too. If you put these 7 Secrets into practice, you will begin to live more fully, impacting those around you with the power of your authentic presence.

Secret 1: BE Silent

Secret 2: BE Present

Secret 3: BE Aware

Secret 4: BE Attuned

Secret 5: BE Positive

Secret 6: BE Connected

Secret 7: BE Yourself

Introduction

"Why are we inspired by another person's courage? Maybe because it gives us the sweet and genuine surprise of discovering some trace, at least, of the same measure in ourselves."
— *Laurence Shames*

In 1993, I had been a full-time psychotherapist in Berkeley, California, for more than fifteen years. As a licensed clinical psychologist with a PhD from the University of California and a successful private practice, I felt accomplished and highly professional. Every day, clients entered the safe haven of my office to discuss the details of their lives: their deepest frustrations and failures, their highest hopes and aspirations. Although my work focused on helping people find, confront, and overcome their anxieties, I had a hidden terror of my own—speaking in front of groups. I rarely encountered my fear, though, because I could easily avoid situations in which I was required to speak in public.

A turning point arrived when a conference organizer invited me to be a keynote presenter. I quickly declined and admitted to him that I was too afraid to give a speech in front of an audience. The man was genuinely stunned. "But, doctor," he said, "You're a psychologist. Isn't fear your business?" I was left feeling starkly exposed and humiliated.

The truth was that public speaking terrified me. Even when I *imagined* an audience assembled, looking at me and waiting for me to say something, my body triggered alarms. On the few occasions when I had to make presentations, I was overwhelmed by unpleasant and uncontrollable physical sensations. My racing pulse pounded inside my head like thunder. My stomach tightened until it throbbed, and my throat constricted. The feeling of strangulation advanced into degrees of suffocation. With these painful sensations spreading from head to toe, there was no way I could connect with my thoughts and render them into words.

What was I afraid of? How had this fear become so debilitating? When had it begun? Could I even recall a time when I was free to be myself in front of others?

Actually, yes, I could. In high school, I had felt eager to lead my classmates. I had been elected to the student council and was the "Commissioner of School Spirit." Friday night football games found me rallying in front of hundreds of cheering students and parents. I regularly gave speeches, led meetings, addressed leaders from other schools, and served on youth panels for district and state governments.

Yet over the years, my ability to speak up gradually diminished. As I continued my academic life in college, the classroom stopped being a place to let my spirit shine and became instead a proving ground where I strove to verbally outsmart my classmates. I schemed to impress professors by raising my hand, offering intelligent answers to questions, and engaging in sophisticated dialogue.

The atmosphere of competition was so rampant that when my responses were incorrect or less than completely articulate, I could sense the silent smirks of other students. Slowly, I absorbed the shame of my ineffectual attempts to express myself. There came a point in graduate school when I stopped putting my hand up altogether, and defending my research in front of my doctoral dissertation committee was an agonizing ordeal. Ironically, at that time, UC Berkeley was home to the Free Speech Movement—a period of political unrest and protests during the 1960s, led by students demanding the right to free speech on a university campus. But I did not feel the same freedom for myself.

By the time I finished my formal education, my capacity to hold forth in public had greatly diminished. Whenever eyes turned in my direction, I experienced a paralyzing unease. I was terribly afraid of being criticized and judged. As my imagination played it out, if someone did laugh at me, I'd feel hurt and embarrassed. If I went blank, I'd look stupid. If people didn't agree with me, I'd feel like a failure. When my mind plucked at the terror, warning vibrations shot through my entire body. "Beware," they cautioned. "You don't have the right answer—and if you do open your mouth, you will sound ridiculous."

I became a clinical psychologist not only because of my interest in human behavior, but also because this profession had the advantage of placing me in an office setting where the focus of attention was decidedly not on me. In psychology, my training primarily centered on the skill of listening, not on developing speaking expertise. One of my teachers used to say that counselors kept themselves polished so they could be good mirrors. You might say I had been trained to be a human blank screen.

From a clinical perspective, it is generally understood that the primary healing component in all therapy models is the quality of listening offered by the therapist. Good listening is good medicine. I followed the prescription so precisely that I used very few words in my sessions, and those that I chose were aimed at redirecting the client back to his or her own thoughts or feelings. When asked about my own life, I expertly deflected the question and turned it into a therapeutic inquiry into what was behind the client's curiosity.

Introduction

My occupation, as I was practicing it, required that I face only one person at a time. As long as I sat in my chair, worlds apart from the public eye, I experienced little discomfort.

Once out of school, I never had to give presentations. When invited to do so, I could always manufacture an excuse to decline. However, I was not a reclusive person. My life included many gatherings with friends and family, and those parties, meetings, and dinners involved social communication. There were innumerable occasions when I had to, at the very least, give an opinion or enter into a group discussion. My reluctance to speak up eventually caused me to withdraw from conversations around the dining table. It got to the point where I loathed returning items to stores because I would have to explain and justify my reasons for doing so. Self-introductions in meetings became awkward; afterwards, I often did not remember what I had said. Even in intimate, safe, personal exchanges, I increasingly hesitated to be open and show my feelings. The fear had invaded all aspects of my life.

The irony of being a psychotherapist who was herself afraid and unable to speak up finally became unacceptable to me. I was shrinking rather than growing. I often received invitations to lead workshops and give speeches, but I avoided them all until that moment when the conference organizer confronted me with that soul-shaking query, "Isn't fear your business?"

Those words finally broke through my shield of denial. I recognized that I needed to explore this enfeebling condition and learn how to empower myself. I felt weak inside and saw that I was covering up. I knew I needed help.

So, help I sought. Over time, individual therapy, relaxation training, speech classes, and Toastmasters all served to build my confidence. An especially significant change for the better in my ability to stand comfortably in front of a group occurred when Gary

Wohlman, the leader of a course titled "Breaking Through Your Fear of Public Speaking," told a story about Michelangelo. When asked how he created his statue, *Angel Holding a Candelabrum*, the great Renaissance artist answered simply that he saw the angel in the marble and carved until he set him free.

Upon hearing this inspirational message, I realized that I had become encased in the hard stone of professional perfectionism. In becoming a psychologist, I had spent years building an exquisite facade, layer upon layer. My essential aliveness, my angel, my Self was buried beneath the weight of advanced degrees and the refined image of being an expert in my field. The opportunity to face the depths of my problem in an environment that was both safe and supportive, with a teacher who could help develop my speaking skills, spurred me to continue in Wohlman's course. I was beginning to see that, little by little, I could free my voice and learn to express myself anytime and anywhere.

Soon thereafter, a flyer arrived in the mail about a workshop on transformational speaking. The facilitator, Lee Glickstein, an up-and-coming San Francisco comedian who suffered from stage fright, had developed a process called Speaking Circles in order to overcome his fear. He found that he felt both less afraid and freer to be himself when he was surrounded by listeners who were accepting and noncritical.

In my first workshop with Glickstein, I could feel my anxiety about public speaking truly begin to dissolve. People in the group listened with a quiet, positive regard to each person in turn. Learning to receive such supportive energy moved me one step closer to functioning well when there was little or no audience support. Practicing among friendly listeners, I began to build the courage I needed to deliver a talk in front of any group.

Standing before a nonthreatening audience that listened without expectations gave me the space to confront and experience my agitation and the impulse to run away. My pent-up tension gradually dissipated when I gave myself permission to feel my discomfort and live through it in the company of nonjudgmental people. Allowing the sensations of fright to speed through my body while no longer having to control or hide them was transformative.

The key attitude I finally adopted was one of self-acceptance. In this new approach, I did not have to think about or plan what I was going to say. All I was called upon to do, via specific exercises, was to stay present in the moment without knowing, caring, or worrying about what words (if any) would come. When sentences did form in my mind, I found that they were connected to my own truth. I began to notice the difference between genuine speaking and words born of anxiety.

In short, the Speaking Circle process worked!

I immersed myself in this gentle learning environment repeatedly. The leader and participants directed feedback not at my words or communication skills, but at the positive qualities they observed in me. I was acknowledged for my innate warmth, humor, and depth; in this manner, those natural qualities grew. I discovered that *a wonderful sense of inner strength develops when the essential qualities that lie at one's core are experienced and affirmed by others.* Improvement was based neither on better speech organization nor on more polished delivery; instead, it was measured by how present and how real I could be.

Since that time I have overcome my stage fright. Now, whenever I have the opportunity to speak, I am confidently myself. Doors that were previously closed have opened.

Speaking Circles proved so powerful in liberating me from my stage fright that I soon began to work with Glickstein and facilitate groups of my own. As training director of Speaking Circles International, I designed programs, developed workbooks, and trained professional facilitators. All over the world, I coached individuals and conducted training seminars designed to help others break through their speaking fears and accomplish their life goals.

After publishing the first edition of my book in 2009, I explored ways to reach people beyond doing workshops and providing therapy sessions. The first edition of this book integrated the work of my formal training as a psychologist, my mindfulness training, and my life's work up to that point. I have since begun developing individual and group coaching programs that have been delivered to hundreds of people suffering from various forms of speaking anxiety. In Chapter 4, I will talk about these programs and other options that I have created.

How to Use This Book

From teaching this transformational process for many years, I have broken it down into the concrete, definable, and measurable sequences that form the basis of this book. By following the chapters in sequence, you will be led gently and systematically through a process that will ultimately bring forth your authentic power and presence. These chapters not only teach you to speak fearlessly in public; they also guide you on a journey of self-discovery.

In each chapter, you will read parts of my own life story. Some of these sections portray my struggle to overcome stage fright, while others convey important lessons I've learned on my journey.

To draw forth your own story, I have designed exercises to trigger your memories and insights. After reading about a particular

Introduction

aspect of fear, you can consider how it applies to your own life by answering the series of questions I pose.

Chapter 1 helps you to explore the origins of your fear of public speaking, reviewing your past and examining any episodes that left you carrying a negative view of yourself as a *speaker*.

In **Chapter 2**, you will delve into your fears about being who you truly are in public. You will learn how you hold back and conceal your discomfort from others. Then you'll examine the imagined consequences of revealing your truth and begin to identify the potential benefits of being more real. The result of this process is finding your own inner strength and the voice that is sustained by it.

In **Chapter 3**, you will discover the *7 Secrets to Essential Speaking* that will release you from fear and strengthen your ability to fully connect to yourself and powerfully engage with the world. As you realize your essential Self, you will tap the power that can transform your fear from the inside out. Because these Secrets are cumulative and build upon each other, it is best to start at the beginning and thoroughly consider the point of view proposed in each Secret before you progress to the next one. At this stage of the process, simply take in the new point of view. The chapters to follow will provide you with instructions on how to practice these Secrets and incorporate them into your daily life.

Chapter 4 introduces you to the options you have to master the Secrets to Essential Speaking so that you can find your voice. Working with me is a direct way to get the ongoing support it takes to face your fears and build a new set of skills. I also suggest you explore Speaking Circles, a method that allows you to go at your own pace as you learn how to speak in front of a group. The other options are practicing on your own and practicing in a group.

Chapter 5 tells you how to form an Essential Speaking Practice Group as a way of increasing your practice. You can certainly benefit from working on your own by following my suggestions. But since the fear in question is about speaking in front of others, you will more fully release that fear by working in a group or with a partner. In these supportive settings, you can more quickly transform your fear of speaking into a powerhouse of natural presence.

Chapter 6 demonstrates the value of Essential Speaking as it applies to your daily life. Imagine being confident enough to eagerly present a report in class or lead a meeting at work. Imagine feeling excited about giving a toast at your best friend's wedding. And think what it would mean for global peace if there were respect, permission, and understanding for all the different voices in the world. I can assure you that you are more likely to be seen and heard if you know how to stay present with yourself and others as you speak authentically. Being the center of attention—once a trigger for anxiety—will become a source of enjoyment as you master the 7 Secrets.

By the time you finish this book, you will understand what is at the core of your fear of speaking: that it is mostly based on the fear of being who you essentially are in front of others. By using the Essential Speaking process to develop the confidence to be yourself in all situations, you will lose your terror of public speaking and begin living every day with an abundance of presence, ease, and joy.

CHAPTER 1

Fear of Public Speaking

"Fear is like an emotional roommate that lives with you night and day."
— Barbara De Angelis

At a crucial point in my life, I turned down the chance to share my story—a story that could have helped others—because of my fear of speaking in public.

At the age of 45, during a routine physical exam, I was diagnosed with diabetes. It was shocking news, and learning how to live with the disease was a challenge. Yet shocking news has a way of motivating people to make changes. Within a year, I had successfully transformed my lifestyle into a more health-promoting one—exercising daily at the gym, eating more vegetables, and reducing stress.

When my doctor first gave me the news, I realized I must have been walking around as an undiagnosed diabetic for months, or perhaps years. Without knowing it, I had put myself at great risk. I was simply ignorant. Since cancer runs in my family, not diabetes, I had never paid attention to diabetes or learned about the symptoms. I thought my exhaustion was due to overwork. The fact that I was always thirsty didn't bother me because I knew that drinking large amounts of water was recommended by health experts. I thought my blurred vision was a result of air pollution. I was not aware that exhaustion, excessive thirst, and blurred vision are all signs of diabetes.

Once I learned to manage the condition, I felt compelled to tell my story, to teach the world about diabetes, and perhaps make a difference with a disease that is the fourth leading cause of death in the United States. I knew I had suffered needlessly and wanted to help educate communities about the symptoms and risks involved. I began to envision myself as a spokesperson for the American Diabetes Association and enrolled in an ADA training program designed to teach volunteers how to make presentations about diabetes as part of a national prevention campaign. After six weeks of studying statistics, major causes, and warning signs, I was assigned to give a prepared talk to the trainers.

At that point, I stopped going to the class and never went back, all because I was too afraid to give the speech. I cringed when I thought of standing in front of the teachers who would judge and evaluate me. I wanted their approval, but the image of those faces staring at me while I made my presentation frightened me into not doing it. I was not intimidated by the subject matter itself, since I was living with diabetes every minute of every day and had studied it intensively. I knew the instructors were on my side. But I could not make myself follow through with the assignment. Also, I convinced myself that if I felt so much anxiety appearing before supportive people, it would be even worse to go on a stage before a multitude of unknown faces.

By not finishing the course, I deprived myself of a very meaningful experience, and also shortchanged those potential listeners who might have learned from my experience. Due to my intense apprehension, I shut down and did not explore a new path of communicating all that I had learned with other diabetics and their families. I had life-saving information to offer, yet nobody received it. No one heard, from my lips, the startling evidence that might have rescued a life. And since no one heard what I had to say, no one was empowered by my individual experience—which might have resonated with many or been exactly what at least one audience member needed to hear.

I had let myself down, as well. In trying to come to terms with insulin injections, new dietary choices, and emotional challenges, I had suffered alone. By telling my story, I might have broken through my solitary confinement and connected with a sympathetic community. Not sharing my challenges and solutions kept me in an agony of isolation.

How Fear Shows Up

The fear of speaking in public prevents *many* people from sharing what they know and from being more of who they are. Every individual is a storehouse of knowledge. When there are communication blocks, our insights and know-how get sealed inside. Everyone loses when we can't articulate our ideas and offer our expertise.

Three women who took workshops with me illustrate this unfortunate reality. Each had been living a remarkable and unique existence and had a desire to tell her story but held back from stepping into the limelight. One, the wife of a murdered underground political leader, was asked by a community organization to portray her involvement with a radical group active during the 1960s, but she was too nervous about her speaking skills to do so. Another, who had discovered a resourceful approach to living with dyslexia, wanted to spread her good news—until her stage fright stopped her short. And a successful doctor who had developed an unprecedented system of managing menopause was uncomfortable before audiences of any size.

All three women were brimming with innovative ideas to share, but their potential contributions were locked away from society's eyes and ears. These creative people could not extend their voices.

What are the ways *you* have held yourself back from speaking? You might ask yourself:

- Is there something I feel strongly about, but cannot express?
- Is there a leadership role I would like to play in an organization?
- Would I participate more actively in the PTA, a community group, business networking functions, or some other kind of organization if I didn't feel so nervous about being in the spotlight?

What happens when a person is too timid to speak? Addressing various audiences can lead to great opportunities, while withdrawal often thwarts any significant outcome.

For example, because one client was too uneasy about undergoing an employment interview, he did not apply for the job promotion he had dreamed of. His long hours at the office preparing for career advancement were about to pay off, but he got cold feet and hesitated. Others, less qualified but more willing or able to speak up, passed him by.

Another client, the best man at his friend's wedding, was so distressed by speaking publicly that when it came time to deliver the toast, he was unable to relate the meaningful moments of their boyhoods together as he so desperately wanted to do. "Here's to John and Linda," was all he managed to mumble.

Another client, who wanted to explore relationship issues in our sessions, did not realize the degree of apprehension he had about being in the public eye. Through our therapy, he began to resolve the problems that had prevented him from committing to his girlfriend and began to actually consider marriage. It was then that his fear of speaking in public surfaced. When he imagined everyone's eyes on him while he spoke his vows to his bride, all he could feel was a cold terror. I realized this was not an issue of withholding from intimacy. It was stage fright—or, more accurately, the fear of speaking from his inner Self.

Many people I have worked with have written books and then found themselves required to go on book tours organized by their publishers. Writing may have been arduous for some of these authors, but it was nothing compared to the difficulty of facing audiences in bookstores and confronting a barrage of questions.

I can point to many cases of unfulfilled potential—lives that could have been abundantly enriched, had the fear of speaking not stood in the way. Too many people make the unfortunate choice to remain silent, avoiding the physical and emotional discomfort associated with public speaking.

Why are people so afraid? I cannot speak for everyone, but in my own case, I was afraid of the physical distress that disrupted my thinking and shattered my composure in front of others. I anticipated unpleasant sensations arising in my entire body and not being able to control them.

How Does Fear Show Up in Your Body?

Like flipping a switch, anxiety triggers predictable sensory responses. The heart beats faster, breath shortens and quickens, knees wobble, hands tremble, the throat constricts, and the stomach knots. This tension can produce a rush of heat, blushing, damp palms, and beads of sweat. Some people become dizzy, lightheaded, faint, disoriented, or confused. A severe headache, an upset stomach, and a dry mouth are also common. All these reactions indicate that the body is undergoing stress.

The sympathetic nervous system is wired to respond instinctively when aroused by a stimulus we perceive as dangerous. When we are afraid, we become alert, ready to fight or run away. These fight-or-flight mechanisms set into motion a series of reflexes that can be either explosive or constrictive, making us feel like a blazing furnace or a frozen iceberg. Whether the threat is real or imagined, the physiological responses are the same.

Such powerful anxiety responses can interfere with more than our capacity to produce words in the moment. This torment can take hold for days, weeks, or even months before a planned presentation, disturbing sleep and contributing to various stress-related illnesses over a long period of time.

Is Your Fear Stronger Before, During, or After a Talk?

People with stage fright often report intense physical tremors prior to a presentation, then feelings of relief when actually delivering the talk. After a few minutes of being with an audience, they finally calm down or "get on a roll." It is the *anticipation* that drives them crazy.

Others feel fine until the moment they *step up to the podium* to give a speech. The anticipation hasn't been unsettling; it is when they come face-to-face with the audience that they lose their train of thought, fumble with words, or go totally blank. Like an animal in the wild about to be pounced on by a predator, when such people stand facing the audience, they are suddenly overcome with fright.

For some, "the jitters" strike in the *middle* of a talk. Speakers may pace back and forth on the platform and deliver words in rapid fire and without a logical order. They might hyperventilate, turn red, and sound scattered and disorganized. They may find it impossible to stand still and be composed.

Still others find that the trepidation crashes over them like a rogue wave *after* they have spoken. They may breeze easily through a talk, then not remember a word of it. They cannot measure the audience's receptivity because they were mentally absent. Having no recollection leaves them prone to all sorts of doubt and torment about whether or not they did well.

While the above "types" are common, many people report that their reactions on speaking occasions are unpredictable. They don't know if they will be nervous before or after a talk, because fear paralyzes them intermittently. These people feel ambushed when anxiety overtakes them like a sudden and powerful storm, reinforcing their unwillingness to speak the next time they are invited.

Are You More Afraid of Familiar or Unfamiliar Groups?

A known audience is often considered even more frightening than an audience of strangers. Standing up to give a progress report to coworkers, one man froze on his feet and forgot the details of the project he had been working on every day for months. The audience was composed of people he had supervised and eaten lunch with, yet being the center of their collective attention unglued him emotionally. For this man, the familiarity with his coworkers added to his nervousness, and he was convinced that he would have been more comfortable with an anonymous audience.

Other people find comfort and encouragement when looking out at familiar faces and are more terrified to be in front of those they don't know. The idea of presenting a simple request for funding to a group of strangers caused one of my clients so much consternation that she did not sleep the entire night before the meeting. In the morning, she felt overcome with anxiety *and* sleep-deprived; the unfortunate combination impinged on her performance so much that her mission failed.

Are You Afraid to Be Seen?

The physical sensations of terror that jolt through the body are difficult enough, but imagining how we will be seen and appraised by members of an audience can be even more disturbing. A public display of uncontrolled emotion is commonly viewed by the individual experiencing it, as well as the audience, as a terrible blunder. An entire range of other reactions can then set in—not only does the inner critic judge any symptom of fear as a weakness, but colleagues, bosses, and clients may belittle presenters who show signs of being unstrung by nerves. Shame can be a serious adverse after-effect of public speaking.

When people have been traumatized in public due to a poor speaking performance, they are likely to be upset and off balance in the future. Their past failures haunt them when they imagine a similar situation. Unable to meet a new experience with a fresh, untainted outlook, they ruin their chances of success. They close down, block their potential—and the cycle continues. Failure begets failure.

Avoid the Fear or Mask It

When I was young, I was afraid of snakes. If the neighborhood boys played with a reptile and I showed any fright, they would taunt me, dangle it in my face, and threaten to fling the slithering object at me. If I cowered, they harassed me even more. Since the only way out of this predicament was to force myself to pretend I wasn't bothered, I feigned nonchalance.

Before I transformed my fear of public speaking, a public audience became far more terrifying to me than a snake. I couldn't conceal my fear of speaking in public. Pretending I was confident when an audience was staring at me proved impossible.

Do You Avoid the Fear?

In general, people who suffer from stage fright feel compelled to manage their fear in some way. One means is simply to avoid situations where it will likely surface. People do this repeatedly. They decline invitations to speak, don't appear at ceremonies, steer clear of classes requiring presentations, and refuse to join clubs or groups where they might ever have to speak.

There are those who don't accept jobs, or even apply for positions, if leading meetings is part of the job description. Others turn away from career advancements that might subject them to public humiliation due to their fear of public speaking. Brilliant students don't raise their hands in class. Competent committee members who have terrific ideas don't speak up at meetings. Dedicated volunteers who want to give their time won't join a program if it involves disseminating information in the form of public talks. To keep safe, these people carefully manage their lives to avoid stepping into any activity that necessitates speaking to groups.

Avoidance is an effective strategy as long as you can anticipate and circumvent situations where you know you will be asked to speak. But life surprises you, and anticipating all of its twists and turns isn't possible. Even if you can subtly steer clear or manipulate yourself out of the center of the spotlight, you may live in dread of those moments where you might unexpectedly be approached to speak. It could happen anywhere—even a moment of happy celebration such as a birthday or retirement party, where all eyes are suddenly turned to you, waiting for you to say something meaningful, as you fumble for words.

Avoidance is clearly not a foolproof safety measure. Sometimes you simply *can't* say no—there is no escape. If your only strategy is avoidance, you are in a terrible dilemma. You may be called on to address your colleagues, your job security could rest on your performance, or you may be invited to honor a friend at a special occasion. Saying "no" could mean the loss of your job or an unwanted conflict in a friendship.

Do You Mask the Fear?

A technique used by those who would prefer to avoid speaking publicly, but are forced by circumstances to do so, is to mask their fear with various strategies. Using a script and rehearsing it repeatedly is one way that people attempt to give a polished, perfected speech. They will plot out their gestures—pound a fist for emphasis or deliberately time a pause for dramatic effect. Their approach is to practice every word so that when they are "on stage" they can act the part. These people are trying to create, and then live up to, the conventional image of a dynamic platform speaker.

But scripting a talk down to every last motion of the head and wave of the arm does not assure that you will remember the words. Other terrors sprout—perhaps fear that you will forget the script and go blank. Even with the aid of notes, your inner doubts warn that you will lose your place. Worse, you could lose the notes altogether!

For someone who realizes there is no turning back and no other recourse but to appear for the scheduled presentation, another strategy is the "white knuckle" technique. Forcing yourself to speak despite your anxiety may be the only alternative. People who are passionate about their ideas know that a primary way to market their work is to make public appearances. They might have to grit their teeth and push themselves onto a stage, enduring the agony for the sake of their cause.

Other strategies for masking the fear of public speaking involve alcohol or drugs. I was attending an anniversary event for a friend, and during dinner several people rose to their feet to offer congratulatory remarks. The man across the table from me downed his full glass of wine in one swoop, and in the same continuous motion stood up to take his turn.

By putting a mask over fear, we present the illusion that we are confident. But this only causes additional anxiety, because then we are afraid of being found out and having others see through our masks. This mask of bravado protects the frightened part of the Self that does not want to be seen. We desperately invest in our cover-ups, but in our hearts we know the truth. It is a false front and we are set up to do it again.

The conventional approach to ameliorating stage fright is to bolster one's outer appearance, to create an acceptable facade. Of course everyone wants to look good, be accepted, and receive approval. People don't want to take the risk of being real, because it is too exposing and frightening. They hope the mask will work to make them look as if they are not afraid. This preoccupation interferes with being in the moment, comfortable with whatever it is you have to say, and confident enough to express yourself with ease and sincerity. The goal of learning to speak authentically is to help you to never need the mask again.

What Causes the Fear?

Those who are afraid to speak in public gaze in admiration at speakers who are at ease in their bodies and who can create a bond with an audience. You might wonder, "What is different for them, and how do they manage to be so confident?" You might then become curious about the origins of your own fear, examining your life for clues. Perhaps there was a seemingly innocuous moment when you were ridiculed or demeaned in public. On the other hand, you might remember a traumatic event that marked the beginning of your speaking anxiety. Dramatic turning points—molestation, witnessing a tragic event, or being terrorized—can leave a person feeling out of control and at the mercy of outside forces. A likely consequence of such an incident can make a person unwilling to be the focus of attention because it recreates a similar feeling of helplessness.

Whether you point to a minor or major event that caused your fear, it remains the same today—you hesitate, and anxiety interferes with your performance. As you read the following section, stay open to exploring your own life experience and let specific memories come to mind.

Childhood

Early life is a tender time in which children are quite vulnerable to emotional wounding. One of my clients recalled playing Little League baseball as a boy. During the last inning of a game, his team was behind by just one run and the bases were loaded. He struck out and lost the game for his team. He felt devastated about losing, but it was his father who shattered his ego. Rising above the winning team's joyous whoops and hollers, his father shouted, "You are a sissy!" The accusation hung in the air for all to hear. Silence fell and everyone on the field stared as this boy stood frozen at home plate, sobbing. Years later, as a grown man, he trembled whenever he found himself at the center of attention. When others focused on him, the alert button was triggered and the alarm blasted fear through his body.

Family

Many people explore the origins of their fear by thinking about their parents and families. Parents who are critical and perfectionists with high expectations exert unnerving pressure on young children who are eager to please. Conversely, parents who are neglectful, indifferent, or preoccupied give children the feeling they do not deserve positive attention. Unworthy in their parent's eye, they later cannot stand in the public eye. When a parent is outspoken, famous, or popular, children might be reserved and reticent to express themselves, having internalized the expectation to match the parent's temperament.

Social science research demonstrates that sibling position in the family can influence personality formation and therefore self-confidence. The stereotypical challenges associated with a child's birth order often shape one's identity. The oldest is sometimes expected to be a leader and pressed to be perfect. The youngest often finds it impossible to live up to the achievements of an older brother or sister. Being the child in the middle and crowded out by more verbal and outgoing relatives can put a damper on one's confidence. An overbearing or sadistic child might silence a sibling, thwarting development as powerfully as any adult influence.

Personality

Much of our personality style is created through environmental interactions and conditioning, but innate characteristics make each person unique. Basic personality disposition can explain, to some degree, the fear of speaking up and drawing attention to oneself. Perhaps a child was born with a tendency toward shyness. Some people do have quiet or reclusive natures, while others are more extroverted.

However, just because people are outgoing and can comfortably relate to strangers does not guarantee their confidence speaking to groups. Such people may be envied by others for their dynamic personality, but they could be just as vulnerable to speaking anxiety as anyone else. One client who did possess a gregarious character admitted that his ease with people seemed to disappear in the presence of an audience.

How people tend to think and behave are questions that occupy personality theorists. They devise instruments to measure traits and categorize temperaments. No matter what descriptive classification you identify for yourself, the fact remains that any personality type can be a victim of stage fright.

Teachers

In my discussions with clients, I've been told stories about teachers who unwittingly contributed to the evolution of a debilitating tension in front of groups. Teachers who force a child to speak or read in front of a class may be unaware of the emotional devastation they may be causing. It is unfair for children who are introverted, but express themselves quite capably in other modalities, to receive a poor grade because they are overcome by their speaking fear.

Any kind of instructor or mentor in a child's life may inadvertently stunt a budding confidence. Harshly critical tutors, for instance, can easily shame their pupils into silence with a demanding or impatient attitude, creating an aversion to learning as well as self-expression.

Performing in public is fraught with potential disasters for young people. Even if the teacher is accepting and the child is accomplished, other variables can't be predicted. In an auditorium, lights can suddenly go out; on a stage, a chair can fall, or a child might stumble while walking across the platform. Adults understand that accidents happen; but to a child, these events can cause enduring and catastrophic feelings of embarrassment.

One early experience that contributed to my later terror of public speaking provides a clear example. In high school, I auditioned for a school play. It was a Greek tragedy, and I was to play the part of a witch. The script had me furtively crouched in a corner when the curtain opened on the first act. The tone was supposed to be dark and somber. As I, in what I thought was a dramatic portrayal of evil and impending doom, crept around the stage, I began to hear sounds of muffled laughter. Then, like an explosion of firecrackers, the entire audience burst into an uproar. This was not the effect I wanted to create. I was so humiliated that I never acted in a school play again.

Peers

During the teenage years, young people engage in the process of discovering who they are and where they want to go in life, struggling to find their identities. Acceptance by one's peers is paramount. To appear slightly different from others can lead to teasing and bullying. Differences are not encouraged. The goal is to be like everyone else. Youths who sport odd hairstyles or experiment in ways that separate them from the norm may be taunted by peers, scarring their self-esteem. Rejections by friends can take their toll and cause insecurities. The boy who feels "different" might grow to be the man who is overwhelmed by fear when he considers revealing his ideas in front of a group.

Work

One of my clients who had successfully led a team project at her job recalled a moment when she felt publicly humiliated. Her boss was pleased with her work performance, and at the annual board meeting he suddenly turned and asked her to say a few words about her project. Since the two had had so many conversations and she had reported to him daily, her boss must have assumed that she could easily discuss it. But with all eyes boring down on her, she went into a panic. She could not think or breathe. She felt heat rising in her body. The only face she could see was that of her boss, who was getting impatient, nodding his head to encourage her, then shaking it back and forth in disgust when she was unable to speak. Later, he joked about the mishap and said she was "struck speechless, not struck dumb." Everyone in the meeting laughed. The episode was a devastating blow to my client's ego.

Culture

One "difference" that impacts the self-esteem of large numbers of people is being a member of a minority community. Cultural backgrounds and ethnicity can definitely play a part in how a person feels about presenting in public. Messages about acceptable behavior are passed down through families and ingrained early in life. Some cultures teach that speaking up and telling the truth is rude, inconsiderate, and a terrible social faux pas. In many cultures, women, especially, must censor their thoughts and ideas.

One woman I worked with remembers being a young girl and sitting with her grandmother, who told stories about growing up in the South as a slave. The lessons in the stories were always about survival and the path to staying alive—which meant learning how to be invisible and not drawing attention to oneself.

Even if ties to one's culture have been broken, unseen bonds may still play a part and inhibit the freedom of expression. If you think this is true for you, then examine the messages about speaking that you heard when growing up. Parents, relatives, teachers, and other important figures passed these directives on to you. Sometimes our loyalties are deeply ingrained; we may still heed these commands in an unconscious manner.

It's not uncommon to absorb the view that putting oneself in the spotlight, or being at home in that position when put (or even invited) there by others, is dangerous, arrogant, or something to avoid at all costs. Even if you think you were not given such messages directly, you may have made a lifetime habit of preserving your essential nature by keeping it under wraps, and so speaking in public may feel like the last thing you would seek to do voluntarily. The rest of this book seeks to shift that conditioned response so that you can be yourself and shine, even with others' eyes upon you as you speak in front of people.

Summary

To be **paralyzed by fear** can damage your self-esteem, shortchange your personal dreams, and limit the amazing gifts you could otherwise offer your friends and community. Trembling, blushing, and sweating are only three of the multitude of bodily reactions you might experience—before, during, and after a talk—that interfere with your ability to present in public with ease.

The attempts you make to **avoid or mask the fear** will not totally calm the anxiety that threatens you. Determining **what causes the fear** is what will begin to truly help—and this requires that you look at many sources: from family dynamics to work environments, from individual personality to cultural expectations.

If you suffer serious discomfort at the thought of presenting in front of others, this is an opportunity to look more deeply into yourself. Perhaps your real voice was wounded at some point in your life. If you are afraid to be authentic with others, rest assured that this book will guide you to a lasting connection to the power within you.

In the following chapters, we will examine the underlying fear that is beneath stage fright . . . the fear of being seen and heard for who you truly are.

Exercise: Facing Your Fear of Public Speaking

1. Write about specific times in your life when you were afraid to speak in public.

2. Currently, where are you most afraid to speak in front of others?

3. Check which body cues you experience when you face public speaking:

    ____ Rapid heartbeat

    ____ Wobbly knees

    ____ Throat constriction

    ____ Dizziness

    ____ Feeling faint

    ____ Confusion

    ____ Dry mouth

    ____ Blushing

    ____ Shortness of breath

    ____ Trembling hands

    ____ Stomach knots

    ____ Lightheadedness

    ____ Disorientation

    ____ Headache

    ____ Perspiration

4. When do your physical reactions occur?

    ____ Before a presentation

    ____ During a presentation

    ____ After a presentation

5. Which of the following problems does the thought of speaking in public cause?

   ____ Sleep disturbance

   ____ High anxiety

   ____ Disruption of daily activities

   ____ Quivering voice

   ____ Fumbling with words

   ____ Going blank

   ____ Losing your train of thought

   ____ Inability to recall what you said

   ____ Self-critical thoughts

   ____ Embarrassment

   ____ Feeling over-exposed

6. With which are you more comfortable?

   ____ Speaking with those you know

   ____ Speaking with those you don't know

7. Check which of the following you have experienced:

   ____ Turned down an invitation to a social event because you were asked to give a toast

   ____ Did not enroll in a class because you knew it would involve giving presentations

   ____ Did not apply for a job because you knew it would involve speaking at meetings

   ____ Used drugs or alcohol to calm your nerves

   ____ Memorized every word of a speech and over-rehearsed it

   ____ Scripted your words and gestures to give the appearance of being spontaneous

8. What are other specific ways you have hidden or masked your fear of public speaking from others?

9. In each category below, describe a negative life moment that you think might relate to your fear of public speaking.

> Childhood
>
> Family
>
> Personality
>
> Teachers
>
> Peers
>
> Work
>
> Culture

CHAPTER 2

Fear of Being Real in Public

"Death is not the biggest fear we have; our biggest fear is taking the risk to be alive—the risk to be alive and express what we really are."
— Don Miguel Ruiz

When I was finally ready to face and overcome my fear of speaking in public, I enrolled in a class aimed at helping people confront the dread that eroded their confidence. Until then, I had distanced myself from distress around speaking in public by reading numerous self-improvement books and studying how to structure talks or carefully script presentations. Eventually, I realized that it was time to step into what really terrified me—talking in front of a group. I knew I had to go where my anxiety would peak, and that meant standing up before strangers and trying to express myself.

In the "Breaking Through Your Fear of Public Speaking" course that I took to enter into this fraught arena, I was awash with trepidation when it was my turn to get up. The teacher, Gary Wohlman, led a dramatic exercise where I got to encounter what frightened me most—a room filled with people looking at me. His first instruction was, "Let your body find a position that feels safe." Without thinking, I dropped to the floor and curled into a tight ball.

He asked me to tell him what I experienced. I said, "I feel safe and hidden, and I don't want to come out." When he told me to tighten even more, I became aware of how much energy it took to keep myself rolled up. I was trapped inside a box that kept getting smaller and smaller, shrinking and compressing me.

At that moment I had an important breakthrough. When my body could no longer tolerate being confined in the imaginary container, a strong inner force burst forth. I pushed against the barrier, stood up, and declared out loud—to myself, my instructor, and all those present—"I no longer want to be trapped inside a box."

As I faced the group, trembling for what seemed like forever, the tension began to diminish. At the moment I broke out of the box, my inner strength, the part that wanted to grow—my potential— rose up more fiercely than my fear.

This daring engagement with the formidable unknown, using a drama technique, was how I first uncovered the true depth of my problem. It was clear that I could not tolerate attention that was focused on me for any length of time. It wasn't about whether or not I had anything to say. I was startled to realize it was that *I was afraid to be seen and heard.*

Other people in the class provided different windows into the obstacles. One woman said she felt an invisible wall between herself and the audience. The teacher held up a cloth sheet to represent the obstruction and, as he had done with me, asked her to describe what she was hiding behind and how it protected her. That evening, people put themselves under chairs, into corners, against the walls, even outside the room. They each allowed the most frightening sensation to take over, acted it out, and gave it a voice until something more essential broke through.

Once we had confronted our demons, everyone in class revealed a more relaxed and engaging presence and displayed a more open connection with the audience. For me, it was new to be in my body without feeling fragmented—disconnected from myself and others. As I stood in front of the group ready to speak, I observed my audience's faces. I could see that people were *listening* to me. I watched their eyes and their facial expressions as I spoke, and I felt surprised at how easy it was to engage with each person.

It seemed, then, as if we all had been hiding something. Initially, I had thought this fear was about public speaking, but it became obvious during the course of the evening that it was related to something much more essential. I came to see that *I was afraid to be myself* in public, and this was true for everyone there. We were all too frightened to tap into our true selves, be authentic, and let others see and hear who we really were.

Fear of Being Your True Self

The inner voice, coming from our *Essence*, is our natural voice. Essence is viewed here as the core of our being. Some might call it the "real Self," "authentic Self," or "true Self." We are each endowed with the potential to speak our truth naturally and fearlessly as our birthright. What is the sound of this natural voice, and what words arise when we are centered in it?

Parents welcome the voice of their child and delight in their baby's babblings. They repeat back their baby's nonsense syllables with joyous approval and the infant has its first lesson in pleasing the grandest figures of all—mother and father. Infants learn that if they speak and others respond positively, all is right in the world. As children move into the classroom, teachers take the place of parents and offer a new incentive system—grades. The As and the Fs reinforce distinctions between right and wrong; grades become symbols of the power held by an external, higher authority to make evaluations about our behavior and to mete out consequences. This process is beyond our control, and we can feel overcome by it.

How we develop a sense of who we are is correlated with how we learn in this society. Since our educational system is organized around learning facts and figures, it is hard to grow up and remain connected to the kind of authenticity we are born with. Young children blurt out their perceptions freely, without censoring. They say what they think, often to the embarrassment of their parents. As they grow up, they learn to dampen their directness and honesty.

We begin early to measure our worth by how well we perform. When I completed my elementary education, I received a medal for being Outstanding Student of the Year. This naturally made me feel proud and happy. Looking back, I can see that I learned very early to find a place in the adult world, which rewarded hard work and achievement. At age eleven, I was already on the track that would lead to a PhD and success in the eyes of the world.

Societal expectations shape children and teach them to suppress their innate voices. They forfeit their authentic expressiveness and begin to be influenced more by outer than inner forces. Most schools encourage children to conform and adapt socially. Shaping students for jobs and relationships is the primary goal, not helping them discover who they truly are.

Speaking from their own perceptions and having their truths be heard can lead to unpleasant consequences as children continue to be guided by societal messages. There are rules imposed; parents and teachers say, "Don't be too loud," "Don't be different," "Don't embarrass yourself or others." Later, these internalized messages function as automatic silencers. Authority figures continuously enforce these directives. Punishing, scolding, and shunning children who misbehave effectively teaches them to conform, or else. This training encourages people to censor, hide, and avoid self-expression—and to suppress themselves when speaking, writing, or even talking to a friend. People measure themselves by outside standards instead of through internal guidelines, until the process of diminishing the Self and becoming less authentic is complete.

Perhaps the drive to survive and the need to be safe and belong are stronger than the drive to express ourselves. In ancient times, our bond was with the group and our survival depended on the group. Perhaps unconsciously, we change in order to maintain this bond, to be accepted, and remain comfortable. *It is these factors that form the base of our fear of public speaking—a reluctance to be real, and insecurity about living and speaking from an authentic place inside our hearts.*

Once individuals develop a style of communicating that is acceptable to their family, friends, and the world around them, they may come to believe that this defines who they are. They identify with the approved expression and abandon the truth of what they know or see. To speak from their core has had negative repercussions for so many years. Words that originated from the essential Self were eventually silenced or denigrated, and the voice that could have emerged from the inner Self did not receive the nourishment necessary to grow.

In order to shift our focus from these adapted means of survival, we must allow ourselves to identify the culprits that silenced us. It helps to name the situations and people who had this effect on you, whether they intended to or not. When you become clear about the true origins of your speaking anxiety, you will be better prepared to overcome your fear and reclaim your real voice.

My Journey into the Real Fear

When I became aware that my challenge about public speaking went well beyond the acquisition of speaking skills, I understood why my attempts to overcome anxiety had not solved the difficulties I experienced when presenting in public. I was studying how to make a better speech, when what I really needed was to explore my underlying fears of expressing myself.

My journey of self-discovery began when I started therapy many years ago with Ron Kane, an extraordinary human being who possesses tremendous insight and compassion. Ron ushered me through the process of dismantling the false illusions and protective layers I had erected in childhood as a defense against my inner pain of having been abandoned by both my mother and my father early in life. I had hidden my feelings of inadequacy behind a façade of awards and achievements. I appeared to be strong to people, but I know now I was disengaged from the natural power within me. My real voice was hidden, and I was terrified to reveal myself.

Slowly, with Ron's repeated confrontations about the pretenses I held up to the world around me, I found my way to a more enduring and essential power within. This was my Essence, my Being. Support from Ron was like sun on a flower bud that was ready to bloom. My core strength took hold, blossomed, and grew. At this point, I began to test my voice in various settings, such as Toastmasters, acting classes, and Speaking Circles.

Toastmasters

At Toastmasters, I discovered that the emphasis was on "performing" a speech and not on developing the genuine nature of each person. Workbooks helped us with speech writing and delivery: how to organize and expand ideas, use the voice, vary the tones, and make gestures to emphasize points. I did well, winning regional and district speech contests. But I was still hiding.

The skills I learned in Toastmasters enabled me to be in front of people quite effectively, though I still had to manage my underlying anxiety. I calculated and timed every word and movement for effect, with hours of rehearsal in preparation for a five-minute speech. I controlled the roiling sensation in my stomach, but I could still feel "butterflies" before I gave the speech. My deliveries were always to audiences whose approval I craved, and my underlying self-doubt was ever-present. After speaking, relief was only partial, because then the self-critic took hold and evaluated my performance. I was never as good as I wanted to be. Maybe I secretly sensed that there was more to speaking with true confidence.

Acting Classes

My inhibitions continued to strangle the words inside me, but I pushed myself into new territories where I could explore my inner terrain. The young girl in high school who had given up on acting because the audience laughed at her was trying to crawl back on stage. The pain of that childhood memory did not stop me from attending acting workshops, where I hoped to open up alienated and unexpressed parts of myself.

Improvisation classes required participants to enter the center of the limelight with no script and no props. Each one of us felt the nakedness of the moment as we followed the instructions for the first exercise: "Stand opposite a partner and silently hand him an imaginary object. He accepts the offering and responds with a spontaneous gesture." During my turn, I took off a make-believe ring and presented it to my partner, who received it and slipped it on his finger.

It was that simple. Just create something out of nothing. In improv, one does not prepare a joke to tickle people into laughter. The funniest moments are those that are accidental; therefore, I learned to tolerate "mistakes" and allow accidents to occur. A complete blunder, it turned out, was more entertaining than a contrived skit.

With the more serious acting classes, I chose roles that brought out hidden aspects of myself. I played a scene from the movie *Thelma and Louise*. As Thelma, I was the stronger, more controlled and together of those ill-fated friends—a familiar role for me, since I was the big sister in my family.

During one scene, Thelma loses her composure, falls apart, and emotionally collapses. She crumbles into a frightened, exposed, and vulnerable little girl. As I played Thelma, I felt the strong defenses she had walled up against feeling her fear. We were alike, Thelma and I. On the surface and to the world, we both acted braver than we truly felt inside.

Exploring my vulnerability and stretching my limits farther, I played Frances Farmer, a creative, bold, and defiant actress who was locked in a mental institution. Society often represses wild-spirited women, and institutionalization is one extreme means to control them. My mother, like Frances, was an exuberant and independent woman who was hospitalized several times throughout her life and labeled manic-depressive. As her daughter, I learned well to contain my passions, live within the lines, disassociate from my own colorful expressiveness, and not give voice to my raw and uninhibited nature. In playing Frances, I discovered how irrepressible one's authentic spirit can be. I vowed then to continue my journey to find the many ways to set my body, self, and soul free.

By investigating these themes of repression and self-protection, I learned why I was so afraid of public speaking: I was terrified to tap into my creative energy and be myself. I had been working on my stage presence, but what I was missing was my real presence, my essential Self. I kept searching for the deeper confidence that would allow me to feel safe, be authentic with myself, and speak without fear in any group.

Speaking Circles

Speaking Circles, an interactive group process that is designed to heal the wounds of the inner voice, finally provided me with the support I was looking for. In a Speaking Circle, a certified facilitator gathers a group and teaches people how to listen and speak from the heart. We are encouraged to "be with" our fears, which everybody in the room has. The goal is to learn how to be genuinely present with ourselves and others while we speak. Performance anxiety is transformed, sometimes in a matter of minutes.

Each participant takes a turn being the center of attention in front of the group. They are instructed to notice and allow the sensations this generates in their minds and bodies. Words are not necessary. The group, in an unusual atmosphere of complete appreciation, demonstrates support by being nonjudgmental and offering genuine positive feedback. One of the keys to the Speaking Circle process is that this feedback has nothing to do with what the person says. The audience listens for those natural qualities, such as "warmth" or "beauty," that radiate from the speaker. Each member then affirms these qualities. In a Speaking Circle, participants can grow their confidence and essential strength by being acknowledged for the positive strengths that already exist.

Instead of working to get rid of the fear, we practice "Relational Presence," a state of non-doing. We are guided to be present in the now with ourselves and others. A Speaking Circle provides time and space for participants to find a connection to their most essential nature. From this center arises a new and more authentic manner of relating to an audience. A person-to-person and heart-to-heart connection is made. Speaking in this way is powerful for the listener as well as the one who delivers the words.

As a participant in Speaking Circles, I knew that I would not be judged or criticized. Finally, it was safe to reveal myself. There were no suggestions on how to improve my performance, because the process was not *about* performance; it was about shining light on my natural strengths, my Essence. I could feel that the purpose of the feedback was to help me find the power of presence that resides within, and to listen to it. The group showered acceptance on my essential core of Being. I felt safe to be with others and not cover up my fear. For the first time, I talked about how scared I was and shared my experience in the moment. "You are compassionate," "You have courage," "You warmed my heart," were the comments I received from the group. I was entirely exposed—and instead of feeling humiliated, I discovered the power of my presence. It was bold, and it communicated more strongly than my fear. This affirmative process completely transformed my self-esteem and shifted my confidence as a public speaker. I now know the sound of my real voice.

Facing the Fear of Being Real

When I coach individuals or lead an introductory workshop on authentic speaking, the room is filled with people who have felt the pain of public humiliation and personal self-doubt. Their stories are different, but they share the same fear. Eliminating or reducing it is the common goal. When they introduce themselves, many participants admit they are taking the first step toward facing the biggest obstacle that has held them back in their lives. Some have made previous attempts with more conventional approaches, but didn't get a chance to connect with their natural voices. They were attracted to my advertisement for the group suggesting that learning to tap into one's true Self is the key to speaking with ease and confidence. My flyer begins:

> Imagine speaking in front of a group: your voice flows freely, your heart is open, your words spring forth effortlessly and you captivate your listeners just by being yourself...
>
> With the confidence to be authentic, you can speak anywhere, anytime.

Some of my students have been pressured to take the class because a boss suggested they improve their speaking skills. Their job advancement might depend on their capacity to lead meetings or give sales presentations. Others have recently earned a promotion and see trouble ahead, should they not be able to assert themselves effectively in a public forum. Motivation to improve for the sake of employment or increased job satisfaction compels many people to turn the corner and walk toward a changed future.

Other individuals have traded their spontaneous selves for a corporate suit of armor, and regret that choice. They recall a time when they were more fearless as speakers. Stuffing themselves into a slot, they have lost connection with their vibrant aliveness. My class seems to point the way back to their abandoned inner selves.

And still others are led through my door by the opportunity to explore personal challenges that have hindered them. Many are already navigating life transitions and are actively reclaiming old ground or staking claims on new territory. Perhaps they have wrestled with the pain of a divorce and now have a strong motivation to challenge any obstacle that stands in the way of their restored independence.

One of my class participants had admired the authentic style of a particular teacher who demonstrated that it's possible to be genuine, speak with authority, and relate personally to an audience. When she discovered that I was her teacher's coach, she made a point of contacting me. She saw an opportunity to develop a speaking style that could help her impact the kind of change in the world she wanted to create.

I've noticed that everyone who has a vision of their life's purpose brings extra motivation to the fight against fear. Some people plan to lead workshops, write books, or become motivational speakers. They understand the necessity of going through a personal transformation because they believe in self-empowerment. Finding the path to true passion and learning to voice their vision lies at the center of their hearts' desire.

People who attend my class soon realize that my agenda is to reach into their fear and gently coax it out. One step at a time, we bring this unpleasant state into the light of acceptance, where we can normalize it and ease the shame. We eventually root out the more insidious fear—that of being authentic—which lies beneath the misunderstood condition called "stage fright." By creating a safe learning environment, everyone has the opportunity to discover the essential Self.

Getting acquainted with the real Self can feel like a reunion with a long-lost family member or a joyous meeting with a brand-new friend. In either case, once you have connected with it, this companion will be there to guide and support you, always, on your journey of becoming a confident and fully expressed individual.

Summary

In looking at **what lies beneath the fear of speaking**, we can see that there exists an insecure part of ourselves that is reluctant to step out of hiding and take the risk of being real. The inner voice is the most natural and powerful asset we possess, yet we hang on to the **fear of being our real Selves.**

In order to tap into and develop the true voice, you must take a **journey into the real fear**, where you will encounter your deepest doubts and uncertainties. It can be difficult, but in **facing the fear of being real**, you have the wondrous opportunity to discover what is authentic, claim your personal power, and transform your life. These chapters will guide you in this powerful process.

Exercise: Facing Your Fear of Being Real in Public

1. Describe your real Self.

2. How do you hide your real Self?

3. What are you afraid would happen if you expressed your real Self?

4. Name the people who discouraged your real voice. How did they discourage it?

5. Name the people who encouraged you to speak the truth. How did they encourage you?

6. Describe your personal journey to overcome your fear of speaking.

7. What is motivating you to face your fear now?

8. What will you be able to accomplish when you are more comfortable speaking in front of people?

9. When you acquire speaking confidence, what personal and/or professional benefits will you enjoy?

CHAPTER 3

The 7 Secrets to Essential Speaking

"The call to complete ourselves brings a realization that we have delayed living the essence of who we are."
— *Marv Hiles*

The sun's first rays cut through the dark sky as I stood at the edge of the Haleakala volcanic crater on the Hawaiian island of Maui. Viewing the sunrise from this vantage point was high on the list of events that visitors to the island were advised to not miss. It meant staggering out of bed at 3 a.m. and driving up miles of switchback turns into the chilly pre-dawn air. Most of us who had braved this trek were wrapped in warm blankets, and we lined the rim of the abyss, waiting like pilgrims in sleepy anticipation.

Abruptly, the curtain of night lifted and the stage shone with bright light. This sunrise was like no other I had ever seen. The dawn was so spectacularly sudden. The brilliance grew stronger on the horizon as the shimmering orb rolled up into the eastern sky and announced the beginning of a new day.

I feel a similar sense of awe when I am with people who are fully themselves. Like witnessing the arrival of the sun that morning on Maui, I am always stunned by the magnificence of pure presence. Those who radiate from their essential Self are captivating and compel rapt attention. Their core carries strength, perfect beauty, and wisdom. Whether with words or through silent communication, such people inspire me to reach into my own soul, wake up my own inner Being, and engage more directly and fiercely with the world around me.

We are all born with our own precious resource, which is our essential Being. It is our natural, primary state of existence that bubbles up continually from the center of who we are. Our Being holds our aliveness and our creative positive potential. We can constantly refresh and energize ourselves by tapping into this crystal-clear fountain.

Your essential Being shines brightly, sending forth beams of light for the world to see. This spark of existence is your birthright. It persists throughout your life and cannot be extinguished. Sometimes we may be overshadowed by others who are naturally more extroverted. We may even dampen our inner fire ourselves, due to insecurity or self-doubt. Though the flame at times may be dim or distant, as long as we have life in us there is a glorious splendor at our core that can be actualized and brought forth into every interaction in our lives.

Since the *state of essential Being is a storehouse of enduring power quite absent of fear*, gaining access to it—rather than merely changing surface behaviors—is the most potent way to gain the confidence to speak in public. Establishing a strong, open, continuous connection to this ever-present source is the key to fearless speaking.

With your spoken words *and* the quality of your presence, you communicate who you are. Those who speak from their essential selves have these qualities:

- » An aura of authenticity

- » A genuine depth

- » Confidence that is experienced by both the speaker and the listener

Words coming from the living and breathing Essence project a vital life force. This is the *being*, not the *doing*, of who you are. This is Essential Speaking.

Tapping into your inner voice means tapping into your inner strength. Once Essential Speaking becomes a natural mode of expression, your life will lead to ever-increasing opportunities.

Living from your authentic Self is the most powerful contribution you can make in your lifetime. When you are speaking essentially, you inspire and influence others. Career doors, whether mainstream or nontraditional, open wide when you are able to speak with genuine impact. When fear is not in the way, conveying information and leading others is unforced, natural, and amazingly effective. Intimate relationships also improve when you increase your capacity to be honest and vulnerable. Tapping into your Essence and being real are skills that can be learned. The process starts quite simply, with your willingness to begin.

Questions and doubts will likely arise:

- How do I distinguish the voice of truth from the voice that was trained to please?

- Do I dare take a risk and speak up, knowing that this assertive act will strengthen me?

Your essential voice may have been silenced early in life; reclaiming and developing it is a journey, and requires a guide. I intend for this book to be that guide.

In this and the following chapters, I describe a process of inner reconnection, charting the way to your essential Being. From this essential core, you can learn to speak with true and fearless joy. You will come to know that your public-speaking anxiety is directly related to your fear of being who you essentially are. When you have the confidence to *be* yourself, you will have the strength to speak with ease in any situation.

Unlike conventional techniques for improving performance, here the emphasis is on learning how to connect to yourself and others in a genuine manner. This approach is grounded in three basic assumptions:

1. *Within each of us resides a pure sense of Self, and this essential Self has a voice.* No matter the disconnection over time, you can reclaim that voice.

2. *You must move toward that which frightens you in order to transform it.* The commitment you make in this work is a pledge to discover, be with, and experience your fear. The 7 Secrets in this book will take you gently through a sequence of techniques and usher you to the end result: the natural dissolution of your fear as your authentic Self grows stronger.

3. *Transforming fear is a process.* I have carefully constructed a process based on the 7 Secrets to guide you to your true voice, which I encourage you to follow in sequence.

The process of reclaiming your essential Being and speaking from that place can be equated with cultivating a garden. Within you are seeds of courage and wisdom that will take root, grow, and blossom in an orderly progression as you go through the Secrets; and in the process, you will reconnect with your real Self. Then the voice that arises from your center, even in the most challenging circumstances, will be steady, clear, and uniquely yours.

The 7 Secrets that follow help you overcome the fear of speaking because they are designed to put you in touch with your own vital potential, the power that naturally exists at the core of your Being. Therefore, each Secret begins with "BE":

Secret 1: BE Silent

Secret 2: BE Present

Secret 3: BE Aware

Secret 4: BE Attuned

Secret 5: BE Positive

Secret 6: BE Connected

Secret 7: BE Yourself

In this chapter, I explain the significance of each Secret and introduce new ways for you to think about speaking. Subsequent chapters provide specific "how-to" instructions for practicing these Secrets and applying them in daily life.

I have also identified blocks to Essential Speaking and incorporated within each Secret the opportunity for you to conquer part of your fear as you master a new skill. In the first Secret, for example, you will explore the difficulties and benefits of being silent. Experiencing true silence dissolves the terror you initially felt at going blank when delivering a speech. When you consciously practice and allow yourself to fall silent, you become comfortable with such pauses.

Some Secrets will be delightfully easy, while others will be more challenging. In observing where you have more difficulty, you will come to know yourself more fully and be able to devote extra effort to those areas.

Too frequently, people are encouraged to "feel their fear and do it anyway." When an enormous amount of anxiety is present, following such a suggestion is next to impossible. In the Essential Speaking process, you will find that approaching fear is manageable when it is broken down into discrete elements. You can build on the exhilarating success of achieving even the smallest gain. Feeling accomplished with one Secret leads to a greater willingness to continue and master the next.

The purpose of these 7 Secrets is to help you strengthen your capacity to be real from the inside out. Remember that the seeds within you cannot flourish without positive attention. The Secrets are organized so that your full flowering occurs naturally, in a progression that ultimately leads to the final Secret, which is to "BE Yourself." At this stage, you will have developed confidence in your Being, which leads to confidence in your speaking.

Secret 1 — BE Silent

> *"A silent mind is far more precise, accurate, and powerful than anything that is contained in the boundaries of rational thought."*
> —*Deepak Chopra*

It was a November day in northern California. Silver Lake was frozen, the tree branches weighed down with snow, and the ground was powder white. Everything was still. There were no speed boats shattering the glassy surface and no canoes gliding over the cold water. No ripples lapped upon the shore.

The exuberant sounds of summer were gone now. In the quiet of this wintry day, no birds called out to proposition each other, no wind rustled the leaves on the trees, no squirrels scratched at the dry bark, no insects buzzed. Nature's summer symphony was silent. Snow had blanketed all sounds..

In that moment came a new understanding. I realized I had never before really heard silence; this beautiful and deep experience of silence existed within me as well as in the world around me. With this realization, I experienced a new depth of Being. In that quiet time and place, I could hear and feel stillness at my very center, and I was stunned by its immensity and power. I suddenly understood that life arises out of the stillness and nothingness, both around and within us.

Silence is foundational, in that it is ever-present and exists even before the faintest whisper. The purity of silence is breathtaking. Like a natural spring, it is pristine and untouched. When we see that any and all sounds emerge from the rich potential of stillness, we can begin to value the state of emptiness. We can see the significant relationship silence has with other states of Being, such as creative self-expression.

We might think that being empty of sound, empty of words, and even empty of thought is a negative state. Our society values filling up any quiet space with sound. We have been trained to value speech, judging others and ourselves negatively if we, or they, don't speak eloquently or "go blank." Being caught in a silent moment can make us feel stupid and ashamed, as if we have forgotten what we meant to say. We are afraid to be without words.

The first Secret to Essential Speaking is to BE Silent and allow a stillness to occur. Its purpose is to help you connect with yourself, to get to know who you are, independent of words. Like the silence underneath words, your silent Being is present all the time. You have the ability to stand powerfully in it. Why, then, do you fear silence? Unraveling this fear will help you discover the pressure you are putting on yourself.

One of the major fears when speaking in front of others is this fear of going blank. The shame of having prepared something to say but not being able to remember the scripted words is enough to make you dread the thought of speaking in public. However, going blank and being silent are not synonymous:

> » Going blank connotes a disconnection from thoughts and words.
>
> » Being silent in the way I am describing opens you to limitless creativity, possibility, and connection.

I once dated a man who was a radio announcer. He could never let the slightest ounce of "dead air" come between us. He showed signs of being nervous during any period of silence by tapping his fingers on his knees and prompting me to answer questions. I would pause, contemplating my answer, reflecting on my feelings, forming my thoughts so that I could respond in an honest and meaningful way. Because I didn't immediately speak, he viewed me as uncommunicative.

Being still can be negatively associated with punishment from parents or teachers who were annoyed by a child's animated expressiveness. In an attempt to control a disruption, an adult might demand that the child be quiet or sit still. Having been told harshly not to say a word many times during childhood can restrict our willingness to speak much later in life, especially if it was an ongoing form of punishment.

I invite you to practice allowing yourself (in a safe setting such as a practice group, which I describe in the next chapter) to be silent and let yourself discover what happens next. It is an exhilarating adventure to go into this emptiness without preparation, to explore a world beyond words. In the quiet inner realm of silence, there exists an unlimited resource of natural power.

I had the good fortune of sitting with a small group of people while Ram Dass, a revered spiritual teacher, spoke. The occasion was the establishment of a foundation, Keeping Hope Alive, organized to help victims of stroke. Ram Dass, whose previously eloquent speech had been compromised by a near-fatal stroke, now found it quite difficult to form coherent sentences due to his partial paralysis and expressive aphasia. During his presentation, he was slow to find his words and spent a good deal of time in silence, but no one in the room felt impatient. He let words emerge in their own time, and when he did speak, the words were like polished jewels, elevated and enhanced by the space that surrounded each thought. His personal power was more clear and radiant than ever, and the power of his speech was heightened by the silence that shaped it.

Those who meditate know the value of a still mind. They work to eliminate the "monkey chatter" of their conditioned inner monologue so they can directly experience their deeper nature. Not only can you calm yourself by practicing stillness, but you can also come to know your own depth.

Writers know that the blank page is full of possibility. The empty sheet comes alive with words that become stories and ideas that fill volumes of history, philosophy, and science books. Dare to be a blank slate, waiting with trust for whatever comes forth. Silence, underneath and around spoken words, will add power and immediacy to your words.

Vivacious and energetic, Patti could talk a mile a minute. She was frequently hilarious, and her bright eyes and broad smile were infectious.

"What an outgoing personality!" people would say. Why then did she come to my program to overcome her fear of public speaking?

As it turned out, it was because Patti always felt the pressure to fill up empty space with words. Her nerves would be on edge if there was a pause in conversation. When she spoke in public, the pressure was even more intense. Her quick wit always came through when she interacted one-to-one, but on stage she sometimes went blank. To her, the silence seemed a vast void, even if it only lasted for one or two seconds.

Learning how to be comfortable in the realm of silence could give Patti the strength to be calm when words were just a little out of reach. Instead of becoming anxious and speeding up to fill the empty space, she needed to relax and allow her thoughts and feelings to emerge more naturally. An audience does not mind if a speaker takes a breath to catch a thought, as long as she stays engaged with them.

When Patti first tried to stand in front of the support group without saying a word, her body quivered with anxiety. With all eyes focused on her, she felt the heat of expectation. She didn't understand how just standing there in silence could give her more confidence. It felt like a childhood staring contest she had played when she was young.

But with a fierce determination, she stood still and felt the awkward moments—and then a wave of serenity soothed her beating heart. It was a new sensation to slow down and be quiet in front of others. She learned that the members of the group accepted her without her speaking. They even gave her appreciative feedback when she hadn't said a word.

It was her Being that "spoke" during this exercise, a natural radiance that permeated the silence and allowed people to sense the power of her pure Essence. She realized that words coming from nervousness were not as compelling as those that came from this peaceful place inside. Finally, she was connected to her center, her source of strength.

Patti now knows that being at ease in the silent moments gives her the ability to be more spontaneous. And it allows her whimsical humor to spring forth in surprising ways, much to the delight of her audiences.

Can we begin to see silence, our silence, as a foundation? Let us be deliberate and practice the act of stillness. Being without words is a new freedom.

Remember! Being Still and allowing silence:

- **Is the foundation for all your words**

- **Accesses a vast untapped resource within**

- **Connects you to your natural power**

Secret 2 — BE Present

"What lies behind us and what lies before us are tiny matters compared to what lies within us."
—*Ralph Waldo Emerson*

When I was a Toastmaster, I wrote and delivered speeches, often winning awards in contests. I crafted words into an organized speech with a beginning, middle, and end. I practiced my speeches endlessly: in front of mirrors, into tape recorders, with friends, while driving, while exercising, and even while meditating. Much of my life was spent rehearsing a speech, often weeks in advance. I visualized myself, in that distant moment, looking at my audience, orating with perfect composure. I could imagine the final moments of the evening, when my name would be announced as the winner and I'd walk to the stage to receive the best-speaker award.

As I have said before, preparation is not a bad thing. However, when I was actually on stage giving the speech, I was not at all present in the moment. I was reaching back in time, remembering those rehearsals of carefully selected words and scripted gestures. Trying desperately to not forget, I did not pay attention to anyone in my audience except during my planned moments of dramatic emphasis: *pause, come to a full stop, look someone directly in the eye, and speak the line in a commanding tone—voice low and words punctuated with moments of silence.*

I didn't measure my success by how much I engaged in the moment with my listeners or whether I made an authentic connection with them. I did not even pause to *notice* if they were listening; I just assumed that they were. There was no relationship, no exchange of energy; there was just my speaking at them. The only part of the "now" I cared about was whether or not my audience would give me "points." Just like when I was a student working for a grade, my focus was always on some future hoped-for moment filled with the excitement of winning.

Rehearsing does have value, but the amount of energy I spent on this kind of activity only indicated how much I wanted to look good and win. I created much anxiety and suffered many sleepless nights by striving to give a performance that would garner applause, approval, and recognition.

In the process, I neglected to teach myself how to actually be present in the moment, with full confidence. Lee Glickstein's book *Be Heard Now!* is based on the idea that in order to be heard when you speak, you have to be present. To be heard now, you must be *here* now! There is a direct relationship between the two. Your presence compels much more attention than your words.

The second Secret to Essential Speaking is to BE Present in the moment. The purpose is to discover the natural power that exists in every moment—and that is you. Without recalling the past or anticipating the future, what part of you is free to come forth and speak? Being comfortable in the moment requires a confidence that you can stay present and be spontaneous.

Fear intrudes on the present because of

» past negative events that you experienced; and

» future negative events that you imagine.

But neither the past nor the future exists in the now!

Years ago, while traveling in Africa, I signed up for a tour that took me to the equator. I wanted to stand on that line so that I could always remember being at the point where the northern and southern hemispheres of our world meet. The guide demonstrated an astonishing fact. We were shown that this line of demarcation was more than a geographical point on the earth. On one side of the line, water flowed in a certain direction and on the other, it swirled in the opposite direction. The enormity of the southern and northern hemispheres, each with huge land masses and oceans, is equal. However, the equator, the point at which they meet, is a precise location that exists between the two.

The present moment has that same quality of precision. Like the current that flows in one direction or another, depending on which side of the equator we are on, our thoughts tend to turn in one direction—toward the past, or in the other direction—toward the future, when we are not fully and absolutely in the present moment.

Why are people afraid to be in the moment? To stand on that equatorial line between the past and the future, fully centered in the now, requires letting go and trusting that the negative experiences from the past will not get repeated. Mistakes, public failures, and humiliations contained in memory can lock a person in the past. If you have had negative public experiences, such as being belittled by parents or teachers, you are afraid that the past will be repeated.

A common defense against this possibility is never to make yourself vulnerable by putting yourself in the public eye. The problem is that life becomes far narrower when you reduce the arenas where you are willing to be seen and heard. You may feel safe temporarily, but your comfort will always be threatened, since daily life can be so public. You may be able to avoid a formal presentation, but what if you are asked a question that requires a thoughtful answer when sitting at a dinner table with friends? With the spotlight on you, all eyes looking your way, panic is likely to set in.

To increase my ability to be open and speak spontaneously in the moment, I enrolled in an improvisational acting class. One guideline in particular increased the sense of safety in the course: In the exercises, everyone had to begin their response with, "Yes, and" rather than "No, but" or "Yes, but," regardless of what another person had said. There was no danger of contradicting anyone, since we were instructed to first say "Yes." We then made up whatever we thought would add to or extend the initial idea. For example, one person would say, "The sky is green," and another person would say, "Yes, and look at all the little green raindrops!" By avoiding the word "no," we were training ourselves to accept whatever came in the moment and respond to it without hesitation or judgment.

Expanding your capacity to be in the now will give you more confidence as you become increasingly aware of your inner well of resources. Whether you are generally aware of it or not, your mind and body are full of natural intelligence and vitality. By being present, you will ignite the creative spark that is waiting deep within.

Ann was known for her exceptionally creative mind and high energy. This combination was an asset when she was planning and directing major theatrical events. As director of the Opera-Musical Theater Program at the National Endowment for the Arts, she was comfortable taking charge and coordinating many activities simultaneously. Ann enjoyed public speaking when she could do it extemporaneously. The problem for her occurred whenever she had to deliver a programmed script.

In her mid-forties, when she was diagnosed with dyslexia, Ann finally understood why reading written words had been so challenging. At last there was an explanation for the confusion and frustration she experienced whenever she tried to give a speech that she had written and prepared.

Ann decided to fully face her condition. Instead of just learning to live with dyslexia, she embarked on a journey of self-discovery. When her attempts to share her personal success with other adult dyslexics did not bring people to her workshops, she enrolled in my classes. Her goal was to learn how to be totally present in the moment when she spoke. When she was centered within, she could tap into her knowledge and strength and stay much more grounded. Her voice, her thoughts, her words became much more aligned once she developed and practiced the skill of being fully in the "here and now."

In investigating the source of her problem with public speaking and confronting her dyslexia, Ann found herself speaking from a new voice within. By staying present and allowing the words to flow, a fresh perspective toward her condition emerged and she was able to reach her audience in a more compelling way.

Ann's book, The Other Side of Dyslexia, *encourages and empowers those who face the challenge of living with a condition that is widely considered a disability. Ann acknowledged her mother for instilling a positive point of view, an attitude that is certainly not typical of most people with dyslexia. She now regularly presents lectures and seminars, talking to groups about the amazing opportunities that dyslexia can offer.*

Being in the moment and speaking spontaneously allow a wonderful freedom. You can trust yourself to be connected to your wisdom and able to summon the right words. In a relaxed state, you can hear your inner Self. When you speak from that center, you will experience your innate clarity and authority.

Remember! Being Present and in the moment:

- **Engages you with your listeners**
- **Brings you fully into the moment**
- **Allows for spontaneity**

Secret 3 — BE Aware

> *"We may have to tune our seeing just as we tune an instrument, to increase its sensitivity, its range, its clarity, its empathy."*
> —Jon Kabat-Zinn

I used to be a workshop junkie. I liked the challenge of learning about myself under extreme circumstances. I participated in encounter groups, enlightenment intensives, and psychodrama trainings. In each of these programs, participants were required to take emotional risks. Confrontations with the leader or other group members were common.

I remember an astonishing encounter I had in one seminar with no one other than myself. In the exercise, we students were instructed to hold mirrors to our own faces and look into our own eyes. I recall peering into the glass and seeing my face reflected; however, the one looking back seemed unfamiliar, almost unrecognizable. Only when applying mascara had I ever looked at my eyes, and then it was to measure and admire the beautifying effect of lengthened and curled lashes.

Staring into that workshop mirror, I was stunned to view a cold, critical, and unfriendly expression. Hard and lifeless, my green eyes looked like slate—no hint of warmth, no gleam of good humor, no shimmer of light flickering. It is said that the eyes are the windows to the soul, but I witnessed no sparkling spirit. There was no opening into the depths of my Being. I only saw dark stones warning the onlooker not to get too close.

The workshop leader continued encouraging us: "Keep looking . . . keep looking . . . don't glance away." She suggested that words might arise. Indeed, I heard myself say to the eyes in the mirror, "I'm afraid of you. It looks like you are judging me. Why are you so nonresponsive?" But the voice of the workshop leader urged us: "Keep looking . . . keep looking . . . "

Then, like water splashing over rocks, my tears began to fall, and then a slight shimmering appeared in my eyes. They became softer, more vibrant, more alive. At that moment, I saw my essential Self shining through.

In this transformational experience, I discovered why I was afraid to look directly at people. What I perceived coming back at me were critical glares—the same judgmental face that met me in the mirror. I was projecting onto others what I was carrying inside. I had always been self-critical and focused on my faults. By learning how to soften my gaze and stay with my uncomfortable sensations in the safe space of that workshop, I was able to connect with a different, gentler, and accepting Self.

It was as if a muddied channel had cleared and surging warmth could finally flow through.

Personal happiness, and indeed the survival of our world, depends on people learning to view each other with soft, noncritical eyes. In the public-speaking arena, many people look at you, and some may well harbor negative thoughts about you. The dilemma is that you must be willing to both see and be seen in order to make a real connection with your listeners.

The third Secret to Essential Speaking is to BE Aware and look at people so you can make friendly contact with others and be available for genuine connection. I don't mean a laser-sharp kind of staring, but a gentle, graceful, relaxed way of paying attention with your eyes. Any nervousness or self-consciousness that you experience when gazing into the eyes of just one person will be amplified when you are in front of a full room. Conversely, the relaxed engagement that you can cultivate when gazing into someone's eyes can also be experienced before hundreds of people.

Being visually engaged with your listeners

- » communicates that you are not afraid to let yourself be fully seen; and
- » puts both you and your listeners at ease.

Whether you are projecting your own fears or your listeners are, in reality, evaluating you, you needn't let the situation scare you. You can develop the habit of moving into and through their eyes to their inner Being, to their positive core. Your noticing others and looking at them softly without judgment will serve as an invitation to them to listen to you.

Many conventional approaches to public speaking suggest that you never look people in the eyes and instead set your line of sight on the middle of their foreheads. Or, if that is still too frightening, to locate a spot on the wall at the back of the room and use that as your focal point. But in making these attempts to calm your fear of looking at people, you sacrifice the possibility of genuine connection.

A more satisfying and relaxed shared experience occurs when you stop and notice who is there in the room with you. Instead of concentrating on the fact that you are the center of attention, you can turn the situation around by actively observing your audience.

In our society, looking people in the eyes can carry nonverbal messages, ranging from friendly and inviting to threatening and invasive. Sexual contact is often initiated by catching someone's eye and holding the gaze. Flirting flicks of the eyelids or moist seductive gazes are seen as broadcasting interest, availability, and desire. Eyes also serve as a way to exert power over another. One darting glance from an angry parent may be enough to control a misbehaving youngster. In some cultures, looking a man directly in the eyes is a direct challenge to fight. Children play the game of dare in which the winner is the one who does not look away. In movies, a character with the "evil eye" is to be feared.

Many of my seminars on overcoming the fear of public speaking are held in San Francisco, and my students reflect the multicultural diversity of that city. On some evenings, a majority of my group participants are from other countries. They might be from Japan, Russia, France, or Mexico, yet all of them gather with one common goal—to get rid of the suffering they feel that is related to self-expression.

By the end of the course, the students realize they all have difficulty when it comes to looking directly at each other. An Asian man might say it is disrespectful, while a Latina woman might say it is dishonoring. But regardless of language barriers and cultural conditioning, they all come to realize that they weaken their effectiveness by not being able to look directly and softly into each other's eyes.

We are all socialized within our various cultures, and we learn the rules of communication early on. However, no matter where we grew up, we feel safer with a friend or lover with whom we can effortlessly soften our gaze and allow ourselves to be seen. The word "intimacy" has been defined by some relationship experts as an act of allowing another to view your inner Self; hence, the word *intimacy* ("into-me-see").

We must liberate our eyes so that we can be more fully expressive and see and receive the support that is abundantly available, if we could only recognize it. There are likely to be a number of supportive people in any audience, but we don't notice their looks of appreciation. We expect harsh judgment, so judgment is what we see.

To create and maintain a more open and continuous connection with the people in a group, you must learn how to be with them, one person at a time.

- » Instead of speaking to the group as one collective, look at a single individual and begin speaking to that person.

- » Prolong your gaze, much longer perhaps than you have ever done in the past, as if you are in a series of one-on-one conversations.

- » Start by connecting with one person, then move to another, then another.

You may find yourself glancing away briefly, either to remember your words or out of nervous habit. Keep in mind that every time you do this, your listeners experience disengagement. It is much more powerful to keep your eyes focused on your listeners. To scan the room, survey the ceiling, or gaze at the floor while you speak leads you away from the human-to-human connection you seek to achieve.

Arnel's eyes darted around the room—he looked at the floor, the ceiling, anywhere but at the audience. During his first turn in front of the support group, he could not make himself look directly at the other members gathered around him. He avoided their eyes, believing that he might be able to keep his composure by doing so. Actually, by not engaging with anyone, he was like an untethered kite. Round and round went his thoughts, bobbing and swaying in the winds of his fear.

It was hard for people in the group to listen to Arnel because they felt ignored by him. By not making eye contact as he spoke, he missed the opportunity to create a connection with his audience. Arnel needed to demonstrate that he was interested in communicating with them.

Partly due to his cultural background and partly to his profession, he rarely looked directly at others. He grew up in the Philippines, where he learned to show respect by glancing away when he conversed. His job as an accountant involved very little interaction with coworkers or the general public, and his daily tasks centered on pages of numbers, columns, and accounts.

Arnel's problem surfaced regularly every month when he was required to present his report to management. His dread seemed to peak the day before, ruining the day and interfering with his sleep at night. By the time the meeting occurred, he was exhausted and terrified.

When Arnel joined the group, he discovered that he was afraid to look directly at people and to let others look into his eyes. He imagined that they would see how frightened he was. To hide the panic, he flicked a quick glance at the group now and then, but he never fully connected with anyone.

Arnel had to learn to steady his gaze and allow others to see him. As he increased his ability to tolerate a straightforward meeting of the eyes, his fear began to dissolve. It was clear that members of the group were more interested in what he had to say. After all, he was looking at and delivering his words personally to each one of them.

Arnel now understands that noticing his listeners is the foundation of good communication. He uses his new skill at his monthly presentations and no longer panics as he prepares his report. Without anxiety keeping him awake, he sleeps soundly and arrives at his meetings refreshed and confident.

How would life be different if we viewed each person as we do a glorious sunrise? Without judging or formulating a story about what the other person might be thinking, can we simply maintain an easy and natural relationship? When we learn to look more deeply, we see our own and other people's natural goodness and positive energy.

Let yourself be amazed when you look into the eyes of your audience. The curtain goes up, and there is a room filled with wonderful light and new possibilities.

> **Remember! Being Aware and looking at people:**
>
> - **Puts you and others at ease**
>
> - **Communicates that you care**
>
> - **Allows for a more personal connection**

Secret 4 — BE Attuned

"To listen is to pay attention, care about, take to heart, validate, acknowledge, be moved, appreciate."
—*Michael P. Nichols*

When I was in college, I took a music appreciation class. Beethoven's Seventh Symphony was our first assignment. During many listening hours, we learned to identify the sounds of the various musical instruments. Like voices speaking, the instruments each projected a unique quality. The soaring sweep of the violin, the deep resonance of the cello, the brassy power of the trumpet—all were clear and distinct once we knew how to recognize them.

I entered the class with no real understanding of the complexity of music. Not only was I unfamiliar with instrumentation, but I was also unable to hear musical themes or follow the variations. I knew that the first and second movements were related, and yet I could not fit them together musically. I missed so much of what the composer had intended the audience to hear.

What I eventually learned in the class was to tune into all that was going on in Beethoven's Seventh. I learned to hear the intricate layers that previously I had not noticed. Before, there had been a muddled mix of sounds, but as my listening awareness grew I was able to identify the true harmonic symphony of music. We went on to study Mahler, Mozart, Vivaldi, and other great artists. The true value of the class, I discovered, was not so much in coming to know the genius of each composer, but in developing my skill as a listener.

Before this class, I had assumed that because I had ears I knew how to listen. Yet I discovered that my listening skills could be greatly improved, and I worked at refining and deepening my capacity. I soon came to realize that I could apply my enhanced listening acumen to all areas of my life, not just classical music.

What I call "essential listening" entails both greater focus and greater expansiveness. You can hear both the minute detail and the totality of what is happening in the moment. Greater depth and breadth are possible at once with essential listening.

When you apply this principle to an audience, you can be in the moment with greater confidence and competence. Tuning in to all that is in the room, enjoying expanded awareness rather than automatically surrendering to fear, can be like listening to and understanding the many layers of music as they unfold.

The fourth Secret to Essential Speaking is to BE Attuned and listen to your audience. The purpose here is to learn to take the focus off yourself and put your attention on your listeners. Many speakers stay much too busy trying to remember their lines or make an impression. Their nervousness and over-concern with Self makes it difficult to be receptive to their listeners.

Typically, when we are in front of a group and asked to say something, we expect the audience to listen. They, in turn, expect us to speak. But there is another way to approach our relationship with the audience. What if we were to pause for a moment and "listen" to them before speaking? Yes, it is true that they are silent; but they will notice that we are paying attention to them and will likely respond. We can

- » learn to notice their responses;
- » detect nuances of emotion on their faces;
- » take in the subtle energies that emanate from them; and
- » in short, listen to their listening.

Now, what if we continued to be attentive to them, even as we speak? How would it be if we noticed our words going out and touching people, listening for how our audience receives them? When we do this, we signal to our listeners that we are including them in the communication loop.

Listening to your listeners is a powerful way to engage them in what you want to communicate. Rather than speaking *at* them, you are speaking *with* them. In a one-to-one dialogue, as you speak you notice how your listener is listening to you. When you speak to a group, you can likewise remain aware of this two-way exchange. People warm up and connect better with you when they sense they are being noticed, and making a point of listening to them listen to you can accomplish this.

When you are nervous about being in front of a group, you may not want to tune into your audience and what they might be thinking—which is essentially what I am suggesting. You may be afraid of what you might "hear." But whether the negative judgments you imagine are really there or not, avoiding this important secret of listening will decrease your effectiveness.

Lee Glickstein remembers the beginning of his own fear of speaking, and relates it to his family's style of interacting. In his "listening impaired" childhood, his father and brother dominated conversations, while constantly ridiculing and ignoring Lee and his mother. In my early childhood, I did not receive the kind of criticism Lee and many other people were forced to endure.

The problem for me was that nobody talked about what was really happening.

I remember one early childhood event quite vividly. I was five years old, sitting in my grandmother's kitchen while my father was drinking a bottle of beer. I could hear a dark, foreboding note beneath the sound of laughter in the room. As I listened beyond the laughter, I heard something that was unspoken. I sensed with absolute certainly that my father was about to leave me and also knew he would be gone forever.

I must have first learned what abandonment sounds like when my mother was taken away to the hospital a few months earlier. Nobody explained to me why she stayed in bed for so long, sad and uncommunicative. In my family, I learned to get information by tuning into what people did *not* say, listening to the spaces around their words.

Now, the act of listening is at the very center of my work as a psychologist. I listen to what people *don't* say, even to themselves. I continuously maintain an open, nonjudgmental attitude. My listening supports and eases my clients into being themselves, communicating to them that they can relax.

By improving your capacity to listen to your surroundings and focus on others with the intention of providing support, you make it easier for people to trust you and receive your message. If you wish to create an open environment, you must become a model of that openness and receptivity. And that means creating a practice of listening as you speak—a new habit.

When I was hiking in the California wilderness recently, I stopped to take in the view of the surrounding mountains. As I rested on a rock, I heard the wind blowing all around me. Then I noticed the distinctly different brushing sound as the wind whipped through the grass. The rustling of the leaves as the breeze blew the limbs of the trees was different yet again. I felt that I was listening to music composed by nature itself. While I continued to rest, I was not trying to change anything about the wind. I was simply observing it and appreciating the different sound qualities.

In a one-to-one conversation, most of us are able to simultaneously talk and notice how the other person receives our words. We can read body language and measure our companion's interest in what we are saying. In a group of people, it is difficult to tune into everyone at once. Developing this skill, however, will dramatically reduce one's fear.

The group was working on listening to the audience as they spoke. During her turn, Sandra complained that she could not listen to people and think at the same time. My suggestion to her was to give up thinking!

Sandra soon realized that when she focused on just one person in the group, it was very similar to being in a dialogue. When she paid attention to only one individual, she found that she could speak and listen simultaneously. The trick was to completely engage in a given moment with a single member of the audience.

Until she first practiced such exercises in a supportive group, Sandra was afraid to focus on anything but the material at hand. The audience terrified her. She feared that if she dared connect with anyone, she might not be able to keep her mind on the topic. Her ingrained habit of not looking at people as she spoke, let alone listening to them, greatly diminished her effectiveness.

I posed a simple question: How did she know if people were actually listening to her? To find out, Sandra had to listen to them listening to her—that is, she had to make herself open and receptive so that she could sense their level of engagement. Then she could learn to "speak into their listening," staying in a listening mode and watching how her words landed in the ears of her audience.

Sandra has come to see that speaking without listening is like throwing words at a crowd and not caring if anyone catches them. She knows that she wants her talks to be received, so she now tunes into her audience before, during, and after she delivers her words. People now enjoy listening to her because they sense that she is eager to engage with them.

Learning to listen to your audience in this way can help to relax you into your own peaceful presence. When you are at ease, you are more available to others. This allows people to feel connected to you, so therefore they want to absorb what you have to say. Paying attention to your listeners awakens their receptivity.

Remember! Being Attuned and listening to people:

- **Takes your focus off of yourself**

- **Increases your receptivity**

- **Encourages your audience to listen more keenly**

Secret 5 — BE Positive

> *"The only lasting beauty is the beauty of the heart."*
> —Rumi

In high school, I participated in an exchange program with a school that had a predominantly African American student population. It was the mid-sixties and the beginning of desegregation in institutions across the country. My mostly white school was preparing for the change, and the administrators decided that a good way to promote cross-cultural understanding would be for selected students to experience life in this other school. My assignment was to attend classes at the East Palo Alto campus for a week while one student from that school took classes at mine.

I was honored to be chosen as my school's representative, but I was also nervous. Not only would I be stepping out of my normal routine into an unknown situation, but I was also concerned about my physical safety. Recently, there had been violence and riots across the nation as the civil rights movement accelerated. The rumor about the school that I was to visit was that some of the students there had knives hidden in their Afro hairdos.

Naturally, I wondered if I would be in danger, but being a positive force for change was my intent. I knew that I had to start by preparing myself. After examining my own attitudes, I realized my fears could inhibit me if I allowed them to. I vowed to enter the week with a friendly approach and to focus on the best qualities I could find in every student I would meet.

I believe that my positive intention was instrumental in shaping the great experience that followed. Had I gone with expectations of malicious behavior, I would have been frightened to even walk down the school corridors. I would have imagined weapons tucked away not only in hairstyles, but in pockets, book bags, stockings . . . everywhere.

However, my commitment to myself and to the exchange program was to stay open and to focus on the good connections I could find. Sitting in a classroom, I did strike up conversations with students across the aisle; we helped each other with difficult homework problems and together we completed team projects. In the end, being friendly created more possibilities for me to relax and enjoy myself. I made new friends, including one who became my roommate in college.

I was later interviewed by a local newspaper about the experience and they quoted me: "If you are nice to people, they will be nice to you." Apparently, I had discovered at a young age the power of being positive. I learned that by being friendly and greeting strangers with kindness and warmth, I was able to initiate conversations from a place of strength.

In public speaking, when you approach an audience with trepidation in your heart, you are creating a negative context for yourself. If your imagination runs tapes of what others are thinking, you may be completely mistaken. Fear of criticism makes people sensitive to even the slightest indication of it. Certainly there are situations where you will be judged, but even in those times you have the power to create a friendlier environment. You can do this by intentionally focusing on the good qualities of people in your audience.

The fifth Secret to Essential Speaking is to BE Positive and look for the best in others. The purpose of this secret is to learn how to refocus your attention from things that frighten you to those that will support you. You will be able to look at people and see a positive quality in each one. They become individuals who are simply with you.

In Speaking Circles, people are encouraged to practice "Essence Appreciation" for each other. We teach that everyone's essential nature is positive and ever-present. The Essence qualities radiate from within. We all have met people who exude warmth or generosity or grace. In others, these qualities may be somewhat suppressed, and finding them will require our patient attention.

Learning how to filter out the surface personality and see directly into someone's Essence makes that person appear much less threatening. This "deep seeing" creates a warm and powerful look in your eyes for all to see.

Like a parent who beams with delight at a child, you can beam a positive light to those in your audience. And just as a child feels the love in the parent's gaze, your audience will feel and respond to such warmth and regard in your eyes.

A retreat program I lead in Hawaii is based in part on ancient Huna teachings, the wisdom passed down through generations of Kahunas, the spiritual leaders of the islands. One of these teachings holds that energy flows where attention goes. What you focus on, look at, imagine, or perceive becomes the object of your attention. And once this object has your attention, your energy inevitably flows towards it.

When you focus on your perception of negativity coming from the audience, that negativity fills the room and may eventually become all you see and experience. Much of your energy then must be spent trying to calm yourself or to race as fast as you can to the end of your presentation. Catastrophic outcomes are just a negative thought away.

Fear comes from fixating on what others might be thinking, perceiving only their judgments, and taking these perceptions personally. It is important to grasp that there is much more to each audience member than an active critic out to get you.

- » Look deeply and without negative expectations.

- » Find the goodness that resides within your listeners.

- » Focus your attention on those aspects.

During the summer months, on those Saturday evenings closest to the new moon, the San Francisco astronomy club meets on top of Mt. Tamalpais to view the heavens through telescopes. I once ventured up the mountain to investigate a special configuration of stars that could be seen only on one particular evening. The faces of the club members conveyed an interest in the details of the night-time panorama, but the instruments absorbed their interest even more. Some machines were simple; others were high-tech, observing and calculating in very specific ways the movements and relationships that occur every evening in the night sky. The extensive knowledge these amateur astronomers had developed was obvious. I wondered, however, if all their knowledge might at times get in the way of simply *being with* the naturally exquisite beauty of the heavens. Could they sit on a blanket on a mountaintop and view with pleasure the twinkling, the shimmering, the spiraling of the Milky Way, or the surprise of a falling star? The magnificence of the jeweled sky, just as it is, can take one's breath away.

I feel this same sense of amazement about people. As a psychologist, I have studied human development and behavior and, like those astronomers I mentioned, I have emphasized the technical details of my profession. In truth, being absorbed with such details sometimes obscures my vision. To look at people and analyze their personalities, or to note the incongruence between a friendly smile and angry eyes, keeps me focused on such outward particulars. But when I look more deeply, I am always stunned by the inner beauty of the other person. To recognize the exquisite Essence of another person is like gazing upon a bright star.

This is how I maintain my positive orientation toward others—by looking for their beauty. I seek and find the always-present spark of goodness that burns within us all. I know I can find something to appreciate in another, and I consciously search out that warmth and light. Even though someone may be critical of me, I know that person also has a tender side. Acknowledging this fact defuses my defenses and gives me a way to relate more gently.

In public-speaking situations, I decide that I will influence the positive conditions in a group of people. I will be the generator of goodwill and create a positive field through my own state of being. Since I am the center of attention, I can generate the positive or I can generate the negative.

The notes from Lani's flute rose up the hill on soft Hawaiian breezes every morning of the retreat. Lani let the music of her soul play, yet she cried frequently throughout the day. She was attending SpeakingQuest: Journey to your Authentic Self, a week-long retreat aimed at helping people transform their fear of public speaking. I co-lead these programs at a healing arts center on Molokai.

Lani, a successful chiropractor from Berkeley, California, ached inside because she knew that if she continued to let fear stop her, she would not be able to develop her career and expand on a brilliant idea—one that could benefit millions of women. She dared not write a book, produce a workshop, or speak to groups because drawing attention to herself was so terrifying.

The path to transformation for Lani led straight to the core of her fear. Allowing herself to experience extreme discomfort in front of a supportive group was the start. Even though everyone agreed to not be critical, she still felt battered by their assumed judgments. She imagined that harsh and cutting evaluations were being directed at her. In her mind, every word she might say was being weighed, measured, and assessed for its value, and this evoked a terrible panic.

Lani's tears flowed into the listening hearts of the workshop participants. She felt the longing to reach others, to share her message, but tremendous doubt stood in her way. Would people really care? She received only positive feedback, but it too overwhelmed her. Again, a flood of tears. It seemed that the affirmations she received from other members of the group didn't erase her negative self-image.

Lani began to see that her problem was her own inner critic standing guard and barring the gifts of appreciation from the group. The words used by others to describe the qualities radiating from Lani's Essence—"powerful," "fully present," "inspiring," "genuine"—were deflected by a wall of her own making. This barrier also held her authentic presence hostage; she could not connect with and express her real Self. Slowly the wall came down, and Lani's natural brilliance grew brighter and brighter.

Lani is now a well-known and respected teacher in the health-care community, standing in the center of her core strengths and speaking with confidence to audiences of all sizes.

The magnetism of positive energy involves both giving and receiving good energy, being friendly, and inviting others to relate to you in the same way. My friendliness is not a fake smile; it is my own natural brightness. Like the sun, we all can impart a warm glow. Choosing to live this way in each moment is a "yes" to what is possible.

No matter the circumstances, you can look for support, open yourself to it, and enjoy a feedback loop of positive regard.

> **Remember! Being Positive and looking for the best in others:**
>
> - **Changes your mindset**
>
> - **Cuts through negativity**
>
> - **Stimulates a friendly audience response**

Secret 6 — BE Connected

"Togetherness can be found among any two people, and it can be thought of as a melody running through the people of the earth."
—*Rosamund Stone Zander and Benjamin Zander*

In the mid-1990s, Lee Glickstein invited me to assist him at an international conference where he planned to train speech therapists to use the Speaking Circle method with their clients who stuttered. Speaking Circles had been recognized as a viable treatment for stutterers, as it provided those who suffered from the affliction an opportunity to be appreciated for their silence and pauses. Stutterers discovered a new and immense sense of freedom when they didn't have to maintain a rapid-fire mode of speaking. If nobody interrupted or tried to finish their sentences, they could relax and let words emerge slowly and naturally, at their own pace.

Near the end of his keynote remarks, Lee shocked me by calling me to the stage to speak to the entire group of 200 attendees. Until that moment, I had not presented before such a large audience. Lee wanted me to demonstrate that no preparation was needed to speak in front of a group of any size. I walked to the stage, approached the microphone, and as I stood looking out at what seemed like a thousand faces, a familiar panic took hold. Much like one who stuttered, I was filled with terror, unable to form words.

Then I saw someone in the audience who seemed to be smiling and supporting me. To find a participant eager to connect and listen was exactly what I needed. It was the same as starting a conversation with just one person. I shared with this smiling and supportive individual the first thought that coalesced into spoken words. I continued in this way, finding another who was receptive and speaking with him, then moving on to yet another receptive listener. By the end of my time at the microphone, I felt connected to the whole group.

It was at this moment, on stage, that I realized there truly can be support in any audience. Perhaps I had been too afraid to look for it before. If it had been there previously, I had not yet been able to receive it. Either I had not trusted that the kindness of my audience was real or I had not been open to taking anything or anyone in. It had felt too risky to pay attention to anything but the words I had to deliver.

Often, fear arises when people stand in front of groups because they are simply overwhelmed with all the attention. It can be difficult to receive so much energy. The way to manage this fear is to focus on one receptive person at a time, receiving their regard as you speak.

Most people are at least somewhat comfortable with one-to-one contact and conversation. It is logical, then, that the way to reduce stage fright is to let go of trying to connect with everyone and relate to just one person at a time, very distinctly. After all, an audience is made up of many individuals. Let your words reach out to each in turn, until you have created a community of avid listeners.

The sixth Secret to Essential Speaking is to BE Connected with one person. The purpose of this secret is to establish a genuine, one-to-one relationship with individuals in the group. Rather than seeing the group as a single entity and speaking to "it," you create rapport by speaking with one person at a time. In this way, speaking becomes natural and conversational, and fear diminishes.

The more you are able to engage with just one individual, the more possible it becomes for a true connection to occur. Imagine that you are flipping a series of electrical switches. You turn on one light and it shines. Then you turn on another, and then yet another. Eventually, the entire group is illuminated.

In the workshops I lead with Lee on the fundamentals of communication, we suggest to our participants that they imagine each person in the audience holding an exquisite crystal wine glass. We then demonstrate how speaking with individuals is similar to a waiter pouring fine wine, one glass at a time. If words were like wine, you would notice the person first, see that her glass is empty, and gently fill it with your words.

Letting your words flow out gently to others requires a soft quality of attention that demands nothing in return. Staring hard at them can generate extreme discomfort.

What I'm talking about is a way to acknowledge the listener who is sharing the moment with you. You can do this by exploring these options:

- » Have a more open and friendly style of relating.
- » Notice and include each audience member.
- » Extend a light, warm form of recognition.
- » Offer a subtle greeting to each individual.

The audience takes in your energetic presence and remembers it even more than your words. Long after they hear you speak, they will recall the Essence of who you are and the kind of connection they felt with you. Human communication is a powerful thing, and being with someone in an authentic way can be quite memorable.

A professional life coach, Robert valued authenticity as a guiding principle in his work with individuals. When he spoke with his clients, his words were sincere and his enthusiasm communicated a desire to make a difference in the world. People knew without a doubt that he was committed to their development.

Robert's problem occurred when he presented in front of groups. On stage, his concern about making a good impression took hold and he became more of a "performer." He deliberately tried to be entertaining. Although gifted with a good sense of humor, his jokes became forced. He told profound teaching stories, but they seemed exaggerated and the wisdom he had to offer was lost.

Robert built up a stage presence to compensate for his lack of confidence. He was trying to act the part of a motivational speaker. The truth was that relating one-to-one was his strong suit, so what he needed to do was simply connect with and talk to individuals in the audience. In this way he could stay true to himself, be in his power, and be perceived as sincere.

In workshop exercises, Robert practiced taking off his actor's mask and dropping his performance techniques. He stood in front of the group, focused on just one person, and directed his words only to that person, as if no one else were around. Then he moved on to someone else and did exactly the same thing. He found that he spoke more naturally and conversationally when he engaged in this series of one-on-one connections.

Using this technique, Robert discovered that he could make a stronger impact on the entire group. When he presents to audiences, he now builds genuine rapport with one person at a time and speaks without self-consciousness. He is president of Fame Enterprises and author of Success is a Journey.

The important idea of this Secret is to create a series of one-on-one relationships within the audience. Do this by finding someone to be your friend. Stop, look, and listen to the natural positive qualities that are radiating from this person, then surround the person with your appreciation. It is like a warm hello, a silent invitation to meet you in the present and join you in friendship. When you do this with a group, you easily create rapport.

Remember! Being Connected with one person:

- **Generates instant rapport**
- **Results in greater impact**
- **Creates a positive relationship**

Secret 7 — BE Yourself

"And something ignited in my soul, fever or unremembered wings, and I went my own way."
—Pablo Neruda

The members of the licensing committee sat facing me, asking their questions and judging my answers. These examiners were evaluating my responses in order to determine whether or not to grant me a license to practice psychology in the state of California. I had spent eight years in a doctoral program at UC Berkeley and two years in postdoctoral studies in order to arrive at this moment. I was approaching the summit of the academic mountain, close to achieving my goal. I was ready to undertake this final challenge and prove my right to this last ascent, to claim the letters "PhD" and assume my place at the top.

To prepare for this exam, I had spent years studying human behavior. I completed classes and wrote papers on theories of normal development and what constitutes abnormal behavior. In clinical settings, I learned how to assess and diagnose mental illnesses, choose treatment strategies, and evaluate outcomes. I had a great deal of practical knowledge filed away in my mind.

During the exam, there came a moment when a question was fired at me regarding the validity of a particular psychological test. In that instant, my bank of knowledge did not open its doors and I could not find the file that contained the answer. As I searched my mind, I became convinced that "Yes" would be the wrong answer, but I was equally convinced that "No" wasn't right. I pondered. I hesitated. Before me, I knew, other candidates had faltered, given wrong answers, and failed their exams. I was terrified, convinced that my future hinged on this single passing moment of choice.

Finally, I said to the testers, "I don't know." I didn't try to make up an answer, nor did I try to look good. I took the risk of being real. I went on to explain what my thinking was on both sides of the potential answer. I must have communicated that I did have a wealth of stored knowledge on the subject. When one examiner hinted at another scale I might consider, I had the information I needed to accurately assess that the test in question was, without a doubt, valid.

I passed.

What I learned from this experience was the value of taking a risk and being myself. The process itself was an initiation. In this rite of passage, I certainly had to know the correct content, but more importantly I had to navigate the difficult moments by myself. I was forced to find my own way. What saved me was not the part of me holding the flash cards with all the answers, but the part that could shiver with fright yet stand and find the courage to be real.

If you are comfortable being yourself, you will greatly reduce the fear of standing before others. People can judge or reject, as they will, but you know who you are. If you don't know yourself, then you have to make it up on the spur of the moment, and the result is often insecurity and anxiety. When all eyes are on you, it will feel like torture to be exposed.

If you know yourself to be a good-hearted person, no one can take that away from you. Discovering and claiming the many parts of your identity and true nature is possible in every moment. Learn how to look inside and get to know yourself. What are your best qualities? Acknowledge and affirm them. Cultivate them in each moment of your life. Claim who you truly are and realize your full potential.

The seventh Secret to Essential Speaking is to BE Yourself. Express yourself in a way that has the ring of authenticity. The power of being who you are and finding your genuine voice is available, always. Coming to know the sound of your own voice gives you a way to access it again and again. The way to compel rapt attention every time you speak is to be yourself, a person like no other. You are a distinct individual, not a canned performance. Whatever your life experience has been, it has made you unique.

In my second year of college I went to a small Midwestern school that was the alma mater of both my mother and grandmother. The appeal of carrying on the family tradition while taking classes in a smaller, friendlier environment brought me to the cornfields of Iowa. My roommate, it turned out, was a woman who had been handicapped in childhood by polio. Barbara was confined to a wheelchair and needed assistance getting in and out of bed, as well as to and from her classes and the dining hall. I was offered and accepted the responsibility of caring for her. I was a sociology major; perhaps that was why I was assigned to be her roommate and asked to be her assistant—a volunteer social worker always there for a person in need.

Barbara majored in music and had to log in hours and hours of vocal practice. Even in the freezing snow, I wheeled her across campus to the music rooms. There she would position herself in front of the piano and open her music sheets, whereupon she would reach down into her soul and bring forth arias that would thaw my frozen limbs and transform any resentment or aggravation I might be carrying.

In those moments of song, I had the honor of being in the presence of a human being totally in her element. This was Barbara's core coming alive, releasing music that lived deeply and passionately in a body that was so physically disabled. In those moments, she was being truly and completely herself, and I witnessed the look and sound of living authentically. She did not identify with her disability; she lived from her true Self—deep and melodic, rich and resonant.

Those who think their defects are on the inside and invisible to others are afraid to stand up and be seen. They imagine that their protective skin is not thick enough, and they don't want to take the risk of being found out. They identify with their weakness, not with their strength.

Living in a world of expectations and judgments can lead to a constant state of vigilance. If you are not secure in who you are, you will perpetually try to please others. When you imagine speaking in public, you scan the room and see nothing but stern judges looking back at you. When you are faced with making a presentation, you will strive to meet imagined expectations. Your self-esteem will be based on how well you did, not on who you are.

With confidence in your true Self, you can stand comfortably on more personal and professional platforms. Without fear, you will be able to

- » speak from your heart;
- » declare your point of view; and
- » give flawless presentations.

My aunt Ruth was a political activist in the 1940s. She was a social work student at UC Berkeley and gave speeches on the steps of Sproul Plaza, a forerunner of the Free Speech Movement that began on those same steps twenty-five years later. Facing serious opposition each Friday at noontime when she stood to express her radical views must have been challenging. More than once, hecklers threw tomatoes along with their insults. Yet, courageously, Aunt Ruth articulated her passionate view about social inequities. I admire that woman who dared to speak her mind in the face of danger, and she inspires me today to express my beliefs fearlessly.

Michael, an ivy-league college graduate with a degree in business, knew that his future career hinged on his ability to speak in public, but he hesitated to apply for jobs because going to the interview terrified him. Michael was well educated, a star athlete, and popular with his friends, yet public-speaking anxiety incapacitated him. No one could imagine the terror that hid inside his mind.

A high achiever, Michael had taught himself to power through obstacles, but the speaking anxiety had him stumped. In coming to my class, he hoped at the very least to learn how to overcome his nervousness long enough to make it through some job interviews looming ahead. The stakes were high, for his career and life direction hung in the balance. It was what he had aimed for—achieving success in the business world. He was no longer a student working for grades; he was now a young man ready to make his mark.

After the first class, Michael said that it wasn't what he had expected but was more than he could have hoped for. What he meant was that he had anticipated a traditional program focused only on speaking skills; instead, he found a program in which he could finally reveal more of who he was and come to terms with his underlying fears.

In group, he dropped his "together" exterior and revealed his vulnerable side. He let go of the shame that threatened his genuine voice. He felt the relief of not having to build himself up for others. He also felt the freedom of being real and relaxing his guard. Without the pressure to perform, Michael tapped into his true inner strength.

What Michael gained was more than just looking good for others; he claimed his right to be himself, speak with authority, and determine his own life direction. After proving his competence in industry, he was accepted into a prestigious graduate program with a full scholarship. Since experiencing the power of simply being himself, doors have opened for Michael and he's eager to continue on his life journey.

When speaking in public, knowing who you are and being willing to speak from that core connects you with your inner strength and becomes your steadfast foundation.

> **Remember! Being Yourself:**
>
> - **Earns you admiration and respect**
> - **Strengthens the message you deliver**
> - **Leaves people fully inspired**

Summary

We are all public speakers. Whether you are giving a talk at work, offering your opinion at a meeting, or sharing your feelings with someone one-on-one, you are expressing yourself. The question is: *Do you feel comfortable and confident being who you are?* The *7 Secrets to Essential Speaking* help you focus on what really matters in any communication—expressing your authentic Self.

1. **BE Silent** – Always start from a place of silence. Quiet yourself. Being comfortable without any words is powerful.

2. **BE Present** – Focus on the current moment. Let go of concerns about what has happened before or what might happen in the future.

3. **BE Aware** – Use your eyes to take in the people you are with. Don't avoid looking directly at them. Gaze softly and let them see you.

4. **BE Attuned** – Listen to those who are listening to you. Listen to yourself before, during, and after your words are spoken.

5. **BE Positive** – Look for the best in others. See the good that is within and don't get stuck on what they might be thinking.

6. **BE Connected** – Be with one person at a time and be conversational. Speaking to the group at large dissipates your energy.

7. **BE Yourself** – The most powerful gift is you. Tap into who you are and allow your authentic voice to come forth.

CHAPTER 4

Mastering the 7 Secrets to Essential Speaking

"You gain strength, courage, and confidence by every experience in which you really stop to look fear in the face. . . . You must do the thing which you think you cannot do."
— *Eleanor Roosevelt*

I always wanted to play the piano, but the thought of practicing never appealed to me. For a brief period of time, as an adult, I did take lessons from a teacher who had also been my music therapist. She had played a significant role in helping me access my grief after my father died. I knew I could trust Linda to be gentle and not expect or demand flawless playing.

During our earlier therapy sessions, Linda would ask me to sit on one end of the piano bench in front of either the low notes or the high notes; then she would situate herself on the other end of the bench. Without saying a word, I would put my hands on the keyboard and run my fingers up and down, searching for the sounds that corresponded to what I felt inside. Linda intuitively tuned into my mood and matched the timbre so skillfully by playing alongside me that the room would fill with rhapsody.

At the beginning of my therapy, I wondered if I could reach any feelings toward my father through this process. His alcoholism and resultant lack of availability throughout my life had made it impossible for me to bond with him. His promises to visit me, assurances that he would attend my graduation, and repeated declarations that letters or presents from him would soon arrive all came to naught. I was keenly aware that I had spent years longing for the attention of the father I had never had.

I found that music was the only way I could access the remote grief lodged in the crevices of forgotten memory. During the time I spent scouting my emotional landscapes in this way, I never knew the names of the piano notes I played, nor did I understand music theory. But whenever I sat with Linda before the ivory and ebony keys, our duets were the finest music I had ever heard.

Naturally, then, when I decided I wanted to play the piano for fun, I returned to Linda. I had felt like a virtuoso in my prior work with her, so I anticipated that I would excel at my lessons. It hadn't occurred to me that I would need to learn how to read sheet music or practice scales. I expected that when I sat on the familiar bench and stretched out my arms, refrains would flow effortlessly through my fingertips from a spring deep inside. To my chagrin, I soon realized that I was incapable of making any satisfying musical sounds without Linda alongside me, skillfully embellishing my clashing notes with melody and rhythm.

Even though I had achieved advanced degrees, Linda said I needed to return to "kindergarten" when it came to mastering a musical instrument. Locating middle C was my first assignment; identifying notes in the major and minor keys and memorizing chord progressions followed. I selected my favorite songs out of an adult beginner's piano book and began practicing. Eventually, note by note, I accomplished my objective, which was to amuse myself and others with renditions of popular tunes.

In like fashion, if you imagine your body as an instrument and your voice as the music, then with time and practice you can realize a style of speaking that is in harmony with your essential Self.

Options for Finding Your Voice—with Help

Working with Me

Unlike practicing at the piano, which is a solitary activity, you can exercise the vocal cords attached to your deeper Self with the help of a teacher or coach. This is what I do—both in person and online.

In these individual coaching programs, I help people go through a transformational process so that they *do* find their voice, so that they *can* change their lives, so that they can step up into wherever they need to express themselves—anything from a business meeting or presentation to a conversation with a friend.

With my guidance, individuals dive deep into the underlying issues. Since I am a licensed psychologist, we can treat the original circumstances that caused these individuals to eventually become afraid to speak up. To actually have a personal guide who helps people move into their fear is crucial in order for them to feel safe as they go on a journey of self-exploration. For anyone willing to undergo this, eventually this self-exploration reaches the Essence of who we are. The Essence is where our natural strength is, along with our brilliance and our power to be who we truly are. This is the authentic Self. To find your voice, you have to find your Self—this inner Essence Self.

I do that with three- to six-month programs that include a workbook, weekly coaching calls, video demonstrations, and email support. These programs can be done in person or online.

You can find out about these programs on my website, https://essentialspeaking.com.

You can also access my social media platform. You'll find me on YouTube, Facebook, LinkedIn, Twitter, and Instagram. You can get instant help by tapping into these free resources, including my tips and videos, and demonstrations about overcoming the fear of speaking.

I also have the *Find Your Voice, Change Your Life* podcast. Here, I interview guests who at one point found themselves in situations where they didn't have a voice, or couldn't speak up, or they weren't supported for having the voice they had. They share their personal stories about what that experience was like for them, including their insights about where it originated—often through an incident, a trauma, parental upbringing, or school. In the podcast, people often talk about their journey to find their voice, which turns out to be different for every single person. I think that's what makes the podcast interesting: everybody has their own journey that they take to find their voice. People invariably find that once they have found their voice, they have found their gift—what they offer to the world.

You can listen to these podcasts by going to: https://findyourvoicechangeyourlife.com.

I also have an email list, which you can join to get weekly messages that offer support and guidance, and help you see that being comfortable speaking is not about making a good speech. It's about being connected to the truth of who you are, and comfortably expressing your truth whenever you speak. You can sign up for this list on my website, www.essentialspeaking.com.

Speaking Circles

I am forever indebted to Lee Glickstein and Speaking Circles. It's where I first stepped into a process that helped dissolve my fears of speaking, and where I eventually found my voice.

There's something unique that comes from being in a Speaking Circle. You can learn about how to be present and connected to yourself and to your listeners. We call this *Relational Presence*. You can find out about this on https://relationalpresence.com.

I continue to be training director of Speaking Circles International, and can recommend professionally led Speaking Circles. I suggest that you look for a trained and certified facilitator who will guide you in accomplishing your speaking goals. Go to https://speakingcircles.com and search the web for "Speaking Circles" to obtain a list of active facilitators worldwide. I can assure you that a professional Speaking Circle facilitator will offer programs designed to transform your speaking anxiety and increase the power of your presence.

Practicing on Your Own

Practicing on your own also is an option. If you choose this approach, make sure that you set up a personalized program and find ways to develop the skills associated with each of the 7 Secrets. Here are some possibilities:

- » Meditation is an excellent path to the heart of silence referred to in Secret 1.

- » Books on positive thinking can lead to the affirmative outlook of Secret 5.

» Psychotherapy can help uncover the nature of your real Self as discussed in Secret 7.

Practicing in a Group

These solitary methods are useful. However, you will find that your growth toward Essential Speaking will accelerate when you practice with others. Even just one practice partner will increase your progress.

If you want to join with others and practice together, you can form your own group to help you find your voice. I call them Essential Speaking Practice Groups. In the next chapter, I give you instructions on how to do that. You can invite friends, family members, or colleagues who want to explore a new style of speaking that highlights one's presence over one's words. Consider advertising in a local newspaper or a community bulletin to find others who want to experience a method that will not only dissolve stage fright but also improve communications in all areas of life. Then come together for regular sessions, study the Secrets outlined in this book, and follow the instructions.

The reason to work with and practice speaking before others in a supportive group is because this is where your body will more likely trigger the state of alarm. This reaction needs to be felt, understood, and overcome. Even though your mind can trust that everyone in your group is available for support, your physical Self is not necessarily ruled by the logical mind and may respond out of a primal fear. The advantage of a safe group is that when fear arises (just as it would in any comparable circumstance out in the world), you will not suffer shame, humiliation, or rejection as a result of judgments made by others.

Allowing yourself to experience the actual symptoms of rapid breath or speeding heartbeat in the moment, even within your circle of support, may be extremely uncomfortable, but it is the key to personal transformation. In this model, you must let the anxiety surface so that you can feel it completely. *When you are immersed in the distressing emotion, then you have access to the raw energy that is a major component needed to work through it.*

In an Essential Speaking Practice Group, you will open doors to the inner chambers that house your feelings. You will also learn to listen to the echoes of your own voice. When the sound rings with unmistakable authenticity, it vibrates through your entire body, much like a bell that continues to be heard long after it has been tolled. At such moments, those who are with you and are truly listening will feel that reverberation in their own bodies.

The members of your group become the witnesses to your emerging Self. Your expanded presence is welcomed into the world by those who are enthusiastic about supporting you and who share a common goal. They identify with your struggle to escape the clutches of an invisible demon, and they celebrate the joy of your liberation.

Summary

To practice the *7 Secrets to Essential Speaking* you can explore these options:

1. **Practice with a coach.** Find somebody you can feel safe with, and who understands how deep the issues around speaking anxiety can go. Make sure the person can focus on what's most positive within you. As mentioned above, I lead individual and group coaching programs that will usher you safely through each Secret and support you as we develop strategies for you to start applying them.

2. **Practice by yourself.** Use the exercises in this book to help you explore your fear. Plan activities that are designed to increase your presence, your positive attitude, and your ability to be yourself.

3. **Practice with a partner.** Find someone who shares your desire for change and is willing to meet with you and practice together. Follow the guidelines and instructions that are in the next chapter.

4. **Practice with a support group.** Gather people who are committed to exploring an innovative method, and form an Essential Speaking Practice Group, using the following guidelines and instructions.

Chapter 5

Guidelines for a Practice Group

"A step towards what you fear is a mile towards mastering it."
— *Matshona Dhliway*

Scientists who study the migratory patterns of geese explain that birds fly in a V formation because this shape helps the flock make better progress. Experiments show that geese who fly in the V pattern can travel 70 percent further than solo birds. The leader does the work of breaking up the wall of air in front, which then leaves a wake of swirling air behind. This flurry helps lift the next bird along. Each bird continues to create a wave that assists the other feathered flyers.

The message to take from these observations and apply to an Essential Speaking Practice Group: Working together is easier and more efficient than working alone. Think of your group as a flock of individuals who help move each other along.

Purpose of the Group

Before you first meet, make sure each participant is clear about the purpose of the group and what is expected. Those who enroll will be taking risks and sharing vulnerabilities; therefore, it is important that everyone make explicit agreements about the kind of behavior that is acceptable. Knowing how to give optimal support to one another during the practice sessions will help ease the already rampant anxiety in the room and ensure a more stable atmosphere.

The purpose of the group is to make it safe for individuals to practice the 7 Secrets and transform their fears about public speaking. This is a learning environment, not a classroom with a teacher who measures each student's progress. The people who come together understand that they are responsible for themselves, but also accountable to each other as they endeavor to expose their conflicts and try out new ways of being and speaking.

Although practicing with just one other partner can increase your competence, your practice group, ideally, should have at least three participants. Keep the maximum at ten, so that everyone has a turn at every session to receive the group's absolute attention. Meeting weekly for four to eight weeks is a good format, but be creative in terms of the length of time you want to meet, depending on the needs, desires, and availability of group members. The duration of each get-together can extend from two hours to an entire day.

Setting Up the Group

When the group assembles, ensure the physical and psychological conditions conducive to safety are met. The internal nature of this work requires that external distractions be minimized. First, secure a quiet and private meeting room where there are no phones ringing or other possibilities of intrusion or interruption, as any disruption will compromise the group's need for a protected and contained environment.

Arrange seats in a circle or U shape. If participants wish to stand when speaking, consider a theater-style format. Beginning is simple: one person volunteers to be the focus, while the others give him or her their complete and undivided attention. The rest of the members follow, in turn. The amount of time for these go-rounds can vary from a minute to several minutes, but decide on the specific duration prior to commencing your sessions and allow each person the same allotment of time. As both a listener and a speaker (though speaking is never mandatory), each person has the opportunity to practice the 7 Secrets. (The next section provides more specific exercises and instructions for working with each step.)

Agreements for the Group

The emotional security in the room rests on the foundation of confidentiality, respect, and non-interference. Everyone must agree that whatever is said will not be discussed outside the group. A sense of well-being is further promoted if a consensus about personal privacy is reached; even within the group, members need to agree that no one will bring up for discussion any subject that another person has raised in any way. In this manner, participants feel free to reveal more of themselves without worrying about being judged, or offered suggestions or advice, no matter how well-intentioned. Surrounded by an attitude of acceptance and permission, you develop in your own way and in your own time.

Instructions for a Practice Group

1. Gather three to ten people.

2. Eliminate external distraction.

3. Sit in a circle, U-shape, or theater style.

4. Give everyone an equal amount of time for a turn.

5. Commit to nonjudgmental listening.

6. Support each other with positive Essence feedback only.

7. Maintain confidentiality.

Exercises for Practicing Each Secret

When I learned how to swing dance, my teacher offered a few words of wisdom to the class. She said that dance was about being in relationship with three elements: the partner, the floor, and the music. She demonstrated the proper position and posture that all leaders and followers should assume before moving even a single muscle. Then she launched into the basic instructions: side to side, forward, backward, and spin. She introduced music only much later in the evening, after we had practiced and built on the beginning steps.

Most things I have set out to learn, including swimming and scuba diving in addition to piano and dance, have moved forward in steps or stages. Even walking, reading, and writing involve sequential learning processes. The *7 Secrets to Essential Speaking* are designed to lead you from a beginner's state of insecurity to an advanced level of self-mastery, one step at a time.

The following pages contain instructions on how to practice each of the 7 Secrets. As you begin the exercises, remind yourself that you are moving toward and into an area that previously has been very uncomfortable for you, and acknowledge that it will involve some difficulty. The resolve to be a learner and the willingness to begin at a new starting point will empower you. It takes courage to reveal your difficulties, and particularly to do this with others. The strength you discover will be multiplied as you transform your fear, step by step.

Secret 1: BE Silent

The goals of this Secret are to

- » be comfortable not speaking while everyone in a group is focused on you; and
- » feel the power of your presence without words.

BE Silent - Instructions to Listeners

The person taking a turn is at the front of the room or in a position where everyone is able to see him or her. The group's task is to provide silent, continuous, and unwavering support. This is not intended to be interactive; listeners give no direct response. The group simply gives silent, continuous, positive attention to the designated person. Do not encourage with nods or smiles. Each member of the group needs to find that quiet place inside and discover the luxury of sitting in stillness with nothing to do but be there for another. When you practice being still and silent as a listener, you cultivate a skill that also will serve you as a speaker.

BE Silent - Instructions to Person Taking a Turn

When it is your turn to be the center of attention, you will be surrounded by a group of people who are looking at you in silence. The difference between these listeners and the ones you might normally face is that they are here specifically to support you, as you will do for them. You have an invitation to stand quietly and experience whatever comes up for you. Unlike a situation where you are expected to speak, here you have the permission to be still and examine your emotions and sensations.

At this stage, you might well feel a flood of anxiety and an immediate pressure to speak, to say something, anything. You may think that people expect you to speak, or that there is only limited time to get your point across to your audience. Silence certainly can feel uncomfortable, especially when all eyes are fixed on you. Up to now, you have most likely been trained that there is a time and place for silence, and that standing in front of a group is not that time or place. In the past, if you were without words, you or others might have interpreted this as "freezing up."

To break through these fears of going blank and losing track of where you are supposed to be in a speech, you practice deliberately removing words from the equation and simply experiencing what remains in the emptiness. You begin to open to your own presence, which is always there, silently witnessing. To connect with this vital source of personal power, you must let yourself experience the fears and explore how they block you from your essential core.

With this practice, you will dissolve the terror that accompanies being silent, and increase your ability to speak spontaneously. From a quiet, reassured place inside, you will be able to stop whenever necessary, find your words, and continue with your speaking. No longer compelled to fill a void, you will discover the feeling of being in charge and capable of speaking from your silent Essence, not from your anxiety.

Summary of Instructions for Secret 1, BE Silent:

<u>Listeners:</u>

- Sit quietly and attentively.
- Give silent and positive support.

<u>Person Taking a Turn:</u>

- Stand or sit in front and receive the group's silent support.
- Explore what arises when you are silent and not speaking.

Secret 2: BE Present

The goals of this Secret are to

> » be in the moment, without the influence of past memories

or future consequences; and

» be open to the here and now with your listeners.

BE Present - Instructions to Listeners

Being present while in your seat means that you are not thinking about anything but what is in front of you, right in the "here and now." Since there is no pressure to respond or interact, you relax into simply being receptive and available. If your mind wanders, you have the opportunity to watch it and bring it and your full attention back to the moment. Like a meditative self-discipline, you engage in the practice of being present.

Notice whenever you begin to go away, and gently bring yourself back to the now. When in the company of other people, it may feel natural for your mind to stay busy evaluating what you are hearing, or even following your own agenda while pretending to pay attention. Release whatever thoughts clutter your ability to be totally present for the one who is taking a turn. Your commitment is to be there for that person in every respect.

In my first meditation class, the instructor told the group that training the mind to stay in one spot was similar to house-training a new puppy. You can lay the newspaper out and put the animal in the middle, but it will stray away and do its business elsewhere. You have to keep picking up the dog and placing it back onto the paper, again and again. Eventually, it no longer drifts off at random; it can stay in one place when it needs to. So, too, can you catch your mind and bring it back to the task in front of you, which is to be an attentive listener.

BE Present - Instructions to Person Taking a Turn

Being present while everyone is looking at you may cause tremendous self-consciousness. The discomfort of standing or sitting quietly, simply being seen, can be overwhelming for some. As you learn to let go of worrying about how you look, what to do with your hands, or whether people are sitting in judgment, you can relax and be with your audience in the moment. In the larger world, organizing your thoughts around a written speech is sometimes necessary, but in this support group you can take the risk of being more open and available without a script. The rehearsed lines are just vocabulary if you are not fully present.

We have all come to rely on our words and what we think they "should" convey. Making sure every word is in order and that the message is clear leaves out the most important element: you, the messenger. As you become more skilled at being in the moment, you will be more responsive to whatever may occur. The lights going out or a member of the audience asking a question won't be such dreaded distractions once you have practiced thinking on your feet without being thrown off balance. You might consider this "dancing in the moment," a state of poise and confidence that allows you to tolerate, respond to, and live through any unforeseen changes in a planned routine.

Summary of Instructions for Secret 2, BE Present:

<u>Listeners:</u>

- Be quietly receptive and available.

- Keep bringing yourself back to the now.

<u>Person Taking a Turn:</u>

- Allow yourself to not know what you will be saying.

- Explore what arises when you are simply present in front of others.

Secret 3: BE Aware

The goals of this Secret are to

- » learn to look directly into the eyes of others; and
- » allow others to look directly into your eyes.

BE Aware - Instructions to Listeners

Keep your eyes softly open, looking at the person in front. Your practice is to keep your eyes accessible, so do not glance away. This is not a hard stare, but rather a gentle availability. If you notice tension around your eyes, you are putting too much effort into it. Practice a relaxed gaze. You are not fixing your eyes on the other participant so keenly that he feels assaulted with a demanding look; you are giving him your soft attention. Remaining in an open, nonjudgmental state allows you to notice more qualities in others. You might see not just the physical features, but an Essence that twinkles through the eyes.

In your seat, practice both seeing and letting yourself be seen. When the person looks at you, don't divert your eyes. Keep them steadily available. Many people say that when a speaker turns directly to them, they feel as if they are singled out, which feels uncomfortable. Explore this response when it occurs and examine what feelings might be involved.

I remember playing with Jazz, my Siamese cat. We would fix our eyes on each other for a long time, neither of us blinking or turning away. There were no built-in assumptions beneath the looks and no interpretations, as there often are with human beings. This same easy, mutual, nonthreatening, and neutral engagement with one another can occur between people, and it makes clear and authentic communication possible.

BE Aware - Instructions to Person Taking a Turn

Your practice is to continually be looking into a pair of eyes. Whether you speak or not, keep a distinct eye-to-eye engagement with your listeners. Linger with each one so you can notice any discomfort you may feel. Are you afraid you will see lack of interest, disapproval, or rejection in your listeners? As you survey your supporters, you will see only friendly eyes. This unconditional regard gives you an opportunity to examine your projections and to discern what is beyond physical sight—the Essence of each person.

When everyone is watching you, their eyes may feel like drills boring into your body. What are you afraid for them to see? This is a good time to investigate what it is about yourself that you don't want to reveal. If those around you are embracing you with approval, how can you fail? Simply be real. When you allow more aspects of yourself to be seen, fewer fears will remain to haunt you.

The ability to look others directly in the eyes is a powerful communication tool that you will possess more and more as you practice this third Secret. People observe each other as a natural part of the human experience, but often we avoid deep looking or hide our own feelings. Since few are able to tolerate a straightforward meeting of the eyes, your capacity to do so will be recognized and appreciated. Eventually, you will come to be perceived as a fearless speaker.

> *Summary of Instructions for Secret 3, BE Aware:*
>
> <u>Listeners:</u>
> - Keep your eyes focused on the eyes of the person taking a turn.
> - Keep your eyes available.
>
> <u>Person Taking a Turn:</u>
> - Always be looking at a pair of eyes.
> - Explore what arises when you stay in eye-to-eye connection with your listeners.

Secret 4: BE Attuned

The goals of this Secret are to

» listen to your audience as they listen to you; and

» listen and speak at the same time.

BE Attuned - Instructions to Listeners

Attuning yourself to the person who takes a turn in front of the group increases your ability to listen. You are learning how to be aware of more than just words. Nonverbal signals, subtle body shifts, and even silence itself contain information. Listen as if you don't know what is being said—perhaps as if the words are spoken in a foreign language—and notice how this causes you to be more aware of other communication signals.

Become a wide-spectrum receiver and let other parts of your body become activated; listen with your heart as well as your head. Can you tune into someone's presence and hear his or her depth of Being? Take notice of the whole person and you will be able to see beyond the words to a brilliance that pulsates with aliveness in every speaker. This is the essential Self. That presence, more than anything else, carries the words to you, the listener.

People who have lost their vision report the profound heightening of other senses, chiefly the sense of hearing. Shifting attention from the visual and primary mode of receiving information to the auditory system dramatically changes the experience and intensity of being-in-the-world. John Hull, in *Touching the Rock: An Experience of Blindness*, writes about "deep" blindness and how his center of gravity moved to the other senses when he lost his vision. Deprived of one form of perception, he found a new axis that opened a world far richer than the one he had known as a sighted person. When listening to the rain, he could sense, through attention to its sound, what objects it was falling on. We, too, can choose to develop our listening acuity—not as a compensation for visual loss, but intentionally, as a way to enhance our engagement with the people around us.

BE Attuned - Instructions to Person Taking a Turn

Just because people are seated in their chairs and you are the designated speaker does not mean that they are actually listening to you. Observe them; notice if they are with you, and assess the quality of their attention. Are they actually receiving what you have to say? The more you focus on them, the more they are compelled to listen to you because they see that your intention is to include them.

This is not about interpreting body language and making assumptions about those who have their arms or legs crossed. It doesn't involve trying to figure out anything about another person. It is simply a more essential mode of listening, perhaps comparable to "sensing."

When practicing with your support group, others will listen to you without distraction. No one will be checking cell phones or making notes. This allows you to stop and listen to the quiet that exists in the room before you even say one word. At first, simply allow yourself to absorb what you hear. No one is speaking; what, then, are you listening to? Stay in a receptive mode and locate in your body the channels that will monitor and record what you "hear." Use all your sensing mechanisms to tune into the totality of the environment, both internal and external.

You can change the entire dynamics between a speaker and an audience if you develop this skill of listening and speaking at the same time. You may think that communication is, by definition, one person speaking while another listens. Like tossing a ball, words are passed back and forth as separate actions. In practicing Secret 4, however, the acts of speaking and listening are conducted simultaneously.

After starting from a still point at which you have noticed those who are in the room, listen to your own words as they arise and as you speak them. Continue listening as you deliver them to one person at a time. Notice if the person you are speaking to is like an open vessel, receiving your message without obstructing it. After you have communicated your thought, observe the subtle signs of comprehension that are indicated by the listener. Again, this is more about tuning in to how a person is receiving you rather than noting a nod of agreement or a smile of recognition.

Remember, you can become a magnetic speaker who attracts attention by the power of your listening. Once you have sparked others' interest through the intensity of your attunement, you have earned the right to "speak into their listening." Then your words will flow naturally through you and into the receptive ears and hearts of your listeners.

> *Summary of Instructions for Secret 4, BE Attuned:*
>
> Listeners:
>
> - Listen to the words and to the stillness underneath.
> - Listen with wholehearted attention.
>
> Person Taking a Turn:
>
> - Listen to others before, during, and after you speak.
> - Explore what arises when you listen to your listeners.

Secret 5: BE Positive

The goals of this Secret are to

» identify positive qualities in others; and

» generate and radiate genuine warmth.

BE Positive - Instructions to Listeners

Your practice during this Secret is to be absolutely positive toward the person who takes a turn, giving unconditional regard. You construct a "judgment-free zone" in which you do your best to ignore any critical thoughts that might normally arise in your mind, or at least allow them to pass through and away quickly. You may not like the personality traits of the man in front of you or appreciate what he says, but commit yourself to finding the best there is in him.

As you listen, deliberately focus on the speaker's positive features and practice detecting his or her deeper traits, such as strength, honesty, or vitality. Find ways to be touched or inspired, stunned by the life vibrating through this other human being.

These essential qualities exist in everyone. Your task is to engage in a search so that you can identify and articulate what is already amazing about a person. Identifying the remarkable energies apparent in others activates them in you. To spot and experience another's warmth will stimulate your own, noticing courage in another will bring forth courage in you, and so on.

The diamond engagement ring I wear on my finger is multifaceted. A sparkle reflects from each cut surface. I regard the Essence of a person as if it were just such a gemstone. With many features brilliantly exhibited, the Essence of each one shines luminously and continuously. I look for the clarity and luster that the "jewel within" emits, and I can find some glint of this beauty in every person, however faint it may be. This practice helps me see an audience as a sea of glittering precious stones; and it reminds me that I, too, am such a crystal.

BE Positive - Instructions to Person Taking a Turn

When you are the center of everyone's attention in Secret 5, your practice is first to receive the support of the group. Let them see and feel your Essence. Based on remembered experiences, you might think the group is looking for your faults—but notice that here there is only acceptance. No judgment emanates from those eyes. If you think an observer is critical, remind yourself that it is an imaginary figment, a fiction you tell yourself, or a projection of your own feelings of unworthiness. If someone is actually unable to beam encouragement to you, you can neutralize any judgment by honing in on the radiant Essence of this listener.

With this secret, you train yourself to refocus on the positive qualities in others. If you are stopped by what seems like a frown or a glare, you are not looking deeply enough. With gentle eyes, probe into that place where a spark of goodness resides in the listener and make it your focal point. Keep interacting with that aspect and you will dissolve the negativity that may exist.

Summary of Instructions for Secret 5, BE Positive:

Listeners:
- Focus on the best qualities in the other.
- Provide positive Essence feedback.

Person Taking a Turn:
- Receive the Essence feedback given to you.
- Explore what arises when you are surrounded with support.

Secret 6: BE Connected

The goals of this Secret are to

» create rapport with one person at a time; and

» stay present in your body and be with one group member at a time.

BE Connected - Instructions to Listeners

With only a single individual in front of the group, the practice of being with that person should be easy, since there is nothing else to interfere. You are committed to simply being available, with and for only this person. You are silent and supportive, offering your pure listening and sending forth positive acceptance. Being in your seat and noticing how you might tend to get sidetracked, whether by your own thoughts or some other minor interference, will develop and enhance your ability to continually come back to and concentrate on just one person. Regardless of the many possible distractions at the periphery of your attention, you can practice returning to the line of connection between you and the one whom you have agreed to support.

When I am introduced to someone for the first time, I extend my arm so that we can shake hands. With this gesture, I greet and acknowledge the other person. A connection between us is established; we have met. If I am receiving a group of people and I want to welcome them with a handshake, I take each person's hand, one after the other. I recognize the individual and initiate the connection, and by the time I've finished, I feel associated with everyone present. By recognizing individuals, I make a deep and more intimate connection with the whole group.

Likewise, the significance of the one-on-one relationship when you speak to a group cannot be underestimated. Take the time to see each single individual as if you were shaking that person's hand. Speak directly to this person before moving on to make your acquaintance with another audience member.

BE Connected - Instructions to Person Taking a Turn

While in front of the group, be with only one member of the audience at a time, as if no one else exists. Learn how to stay with that person long enough to sense the relationship the two of you share in the moment. Like plugging into a socket, make a direct connection and let the electricity flow. The more you do this, the more powerful the listening experience becomes for the entire group.

Have a conversation with a single individual, then with another. Do this over and over as you speak, and you will master the skill of creating rapport with an audience.

Summary of instructions for Secret 6, BE Connected:

<u>Listeners:</u>
- Be receptive.
- Open yourself to the connection that already exists.

<u>Person Taking a Turn:</u>
- Be with one person at a time.
- Explore what arises when you linger with just one person.

Secret 7: BE Yourself

The goals of this Secret are to

> » be able to express yourself with confidence; and

> » be able to inspire and influence others by being yourself.

BE Yourself - Instructions to Listeners

As you sit in your seat, nothing is being asked of you but to stay open and engaged. When you shift your attention from your own thoughts and concerns, it is easier to relax and simply be present. By practicing the other Secrets, you've developed the inner strength to be quietly present in the moment. You have an increased capacity to be available to others without expectation; in fact, you give thoughtful responses and you offer appreciative feedback with grace. You are learning to tune into and tap into your own deeper Self, where your innate power awaits activation.

BE Yourself - Instructions to Person Taking a Turn

At this point, you will have gained the ability to stand in front of others without the blocks that previously held you back. Now you allow yourself to explore what it means to let words emerge that are wholly authentic. Listen fully to yourself. What do you hear? With the critical voices stilled, find the congruence between what you want to say and the true expression that matches it—where you, your thoughts, and your words become one. With the confidence to be yourself in the moment, you are living and actualizing your potential.

Summary of Instructions for Secret 7, BE Yourself:

Listeners:

- Simply stay open and engaged.
- Give others permission to be who they are.

Person Taking a Turn:

- Listen to yourself.
- Explore what arises when you feel confident expressing yourself.

From Practice to Mastery

After practicing and mastering the 7 Secrets, you will possess two major communication tools that open and strengthen the channel between you and others: *connection* and *engagement*.

Connection

Much like a telephone line that must be plugged in to work properly, you need to be connected to those who are listening. Even in the case of wireless technology, the lines between a sender and receiver interface. Making a connection through your eyes, listening to others, and being present invites them to connect with you in return.

A telephone line cuts off when one person hangs up. Similarly, the invisible networks that link human beings are broken when someone consciously or unconsciously disengages. Like hanging up a receiver, communication is thwarted when one person becomes preoccupied during a conversation. You can feel it when another has momentarily "tuned out" and you are left carrying on a conversation by yourself. "Hello . . . is anyone there?" you might inquire, not understanding what caused the other person to detach.

If you disassociate when you are the *speaker*, perhaps anxiety is playing a part. In fact, you can sometimes measure how much fear is present by how much disconnection you experience. Do you momentarily go to the storage cabinet in your mind to retrieve a thought, or leave your body altogether? Fear has a way of permeating every cell, like a toxin that spreads and inflames, altering our ability to respond in a calm fashion.

Drifting away from being with one person as you speak to a group is a warning sign; but with full mastery of the 7 Secrets, you can come back in an instant. Remember that we all, in reality, live our lives within a web of human connections. To relocate your real Self in the moment, find one audience member to be your listening partner and simply take a breath while you stop, look, and listen to that individual as you would in a private conversation.

Engagement

Once you have the communication line connected, mastery of the 7 Secrets leads you to yet another competency—engagement, which speaks to the quality of your connection. Again, consider the telephone. When a line has static noise, it is much harder—or impossible—to hear the speaker's words. A clear channel, on the other hand, fosters an exchange of energy, whether verbal or nonverbal.

What are the qualities that indicate an open and clear line? How do you establish these conditions? For full engagement, bring into play all 7 Secrets:

- Be *silent* to dissolve unnecessary internal chattering.
- Stay *present* so you can be fully available.
- Open your eyes and be *aware* of the receiver.
- Listen and be *attuned* in order to enhance reception.
- Eliminate negative interference by being *positive* in your approach.
- *Connect* with one person at a time to deepen the channel.
- Finally, be *yourself*, and you will powerfully impact your listeners as you deliver your words.

Summary

An **Essential Speaking Practice Group** provides the best supportive learning environment you need to master the 7 Secrets. Meet together with a partner or gather with others who want to overcome their fear of speaking, and follow the **Guidelines for a Practice Group**. The primary instructions are designed to create a safe zone in which fear can emerge without anyone judging it. Absolute positive listening and feedback that focuses on one's essential strengths are the keys to transforming the fear.

Exercises for practicing each Secret are given, along with easy directions that you and your partner or the members of the group can follow. In short, the listeners do most of the work by giving a high quality of attention, while the person taking a turn explores being the center of attention. Going from **practice to mastery** is achieved when you can maintain full engagement and connection with Self and others.

CHAPTER 6

Essential Speaking in Daily Life

"As we let our own light shine, we unconsciously give other people permission to do the same. As we are liberated from our own fear, our presence automatically liberates others."
— *Marianne Williamson*

If you have anxiety about speaking in public, you may carry this anxiety about expressing yourself into all areas of your life. However, if you find and learn how to access your real voice, then you are empowered to speak your truth in your daily life.

Essential Speaking to Yourself

Essential Speaking in daily life begins within your own mind. What do you say to yourself as you go through your day? Are you even listening to the "voice" that speaks in your head as your thoughts? Begin to pay attention to these thoughts and you will discover the quality of your self-talk.

Negative self-talk erodes your confidence and destroys your ability to be authentic. Critical remarks—"You'll never be good enough," "No one cares about what you say," "You'll always lose"—only lead to despair. Self-esteem suffers with each blow from this harsh mental voice, and procrastination, isolation, and depression eventually set in. Suicide, the ultimate attack on the Self, is sometimes viewed as the only escape from the unforgiving inner critic, forever pointing out one's failures and faults.

In my private practice, I meet men and women who have entered therapy to work on their life problems. They often blame their difficulties on a spouse, boss, or other external conditions. However, when I explore the relationship that each client has with his or her essential Self, I see where the real work must begin.

A positive life is based on the way you treat yourself in thought, word, and deed. Affirmative self-talk is quite empowering.

- Are you supportive, kind, and gentle with yourself?

- Are you able to say, "I deserve positive attention from others" and believe it?

Remember how it lifts your spirits when someone acknowledges your good qualities, and find ways to give yourself this same kind of acceptance and appreciation.

It is possible to practice the 7 Secrets with the purpose of developing a more essential and positive relationship with yourself. This inner journey starts with the first Secret that you have already come to know: **BE Silent**. Sit quietly and do nothing, even for five minutes. You don't have to formally meditate; just be still and take full breaths. With continual practice, this expands your inner state of calm.

The second Secret, **BE Present**, can be attained at any moment. The only guideline is to put your intention on continually refocusing back to the now. You might try eating a piece of fruit and being in the moment with each bite, or taking a walk and being aware of your feet moving and your hands swinging at your sides.

Practice the third Secret, **BE Aware**, when you observe the world that surrounds you. This new seeing is one of innocence. Pretend that you don't have names for anything you look at. Without labeling, simply notice shapes, colors, textures, and patterns. A building is angular, the pond is shiny, and the rock is marbled. Doing this practice, you will re-discover the delight found in everyday moments of first and new encounters.

BE Attuned, the fourth Secret, is carried out in the same fresh way that you approached seeing. Tune into the sounds of life. From the horns and engines of traffic to the rhythmic waves of the ocean, a constant cacophony of tones washes over us. Let in the noises without identifying what you hear. Also, fine-tune your inner ear and listen to your thoughts and feelings. Let them be as they are; don't try to interpret or change them. Practice listening for the wise voice that guides and counsels you, and eventually you will hear it.

Actively practice the fifth Secret, **BE Positive**, by continuously blessing the world around you. You don't have to be a monk to live spiritual principles. Simply being grateful is a profound spiritual act. A Buddhist saying tells people to "practice random acts of kindness and senseless acts of beauty."

When you practice the sixth Secret, **BE Connected**, visualize an electrical current between you and your essential Self. If you disengage, you are cutting yourself off from your own natural energy source. With direct and unlimited access to this boundless resource, you are able to leap over hurdles and move fearlessly toward your goals. Extend this connective line to the heart of everyone you meet, and you will discover that we are all part of one web of life.

When you realize the power to **BE Yourself**, the promise of Secret seven, you confidently live every minute of every day. Your authentic inner voice will guide you through obstacles and usher you to your dreams. You might notice that when you begin voicing your opinions at work, you finally receive the recognition and promotion you've deserved. Or you might leave your job and invent an entirely new career that brings you great fulfillment. Expressing your needs for more affection may bring you and your partner to new levels of intimacy.

When you can speak to yourself with a positive regard, feel the truth of a self-affirmation, and listen to the voice of compassionate self-care, then you are practicing Essential Speaking with yourself. These conscious acts will produce an internal support system that will keep you strong even when things seem to fall apart.

> Remember to apply the *7 Secrets to Essential Speaking* to yourself:
>
> - **Sit quietly again and again.**
> - **Continually re-focus on the now.**
> - **See with fresh and innocent eyes.**
> - **Listen as if for the first time.**
> - **Bless every moment.**
> - **Know that we are all part of one connected web.**
> - **Let your authentic voice thrive.**

Essential Speaking with Family

With the skills you master in the 7 Secrets, you can more easily find a love relationship because you have an elegant and sophisticated instrument—your essential Self—to guide you. If you are already coupled, you will be able to engage more deeply with your partner. When you improve your style of communication and are more present, your entire family, including your children, will notice the difference and appreciate the new connection they feel.

In looking for a relationship, men and women usually start with a mental ideal. They list personality traits, education and income levels, appearance, and other qualities that they imagine will fulfill their fantasies. Mate selection done consciously is something new in our society, and matchmaking services are now big business. Yet this approach keeps things on a superficial level. The trick is not so much picking a person who fits your wish list; rather, it is recognizing in an essential way the right person when he or she comes along.

If you evaluate people on the basis of more significant and enduring qualities, you are able to recognize their *essential* Selves. Many questions can help you recognize the deeper levels:

- What positive qualities does this person radiate naturally?

- Does he listen to you attentively?

- Does she acknowledge and affirm you and others?

Of course, to create a healthy relationship, you have to be healthy yourself. Before you can recognize another's essential Self, you must already be in touch with your own. The 7 Secrets outlined in this book are designed with just this goal in mind.

If you have developed your ability to speak from your heart, even the word "hello" will vibrate with genuine warmth and communicate sincerity. Being fully yourself, you can trust that your natural attractiveness will be a magnet for the best mate for you. When you are yourself, you attract the kind of person who truly wants to be around you, and perhaps it will lead to a lifetime of togetherness. When you are trying to attract others by putting on false appearances, you are doomed to disappointment and heartbreak.

Those who remain with their partners even when they know it is not good for them have their own reasons for doing so. They tell themselves that things might get better, or they feel stuck and incapable of creating other options. Children who are young and need parental care are sometimes enough of a rationale for a person to stay in a relationship long after the bonds have been broken. An abusive relationship can be hard to break out of because one spouse believes that as soon as this particular violent episode ends, there will be a return to "normal" life.

Many people weigh all the pleasant and disagreeable aspects of their relationships and conclude that it is best to persist. Whether it is for the intermittent love or financial security, or it is driven by the fear of being alone, they choose to continue in relationships where honesty and true intimacy are rare or completely absent. In such cases, the children in the family often suffer negative consequences, trapped in a household with unhappy adults.

Improving a relationship that is faltering and bringing a family into more harmony is possible by practicing the 7 Secrets *together*. The mutual commitment to accomplish change is a powerful declaration. With either your partner or all members of the family in agreement, arrange to meet just once or on a more regular basis for a certain number of weeks. Allow at least an hour for this session. Turn off phones and sit in a circle, or face each other if there are just two of you.

The first Secret, **BE Silent**, done with conscious intention, will allow a couple or a family to share a new aspect of their relationship. Unlike the "silent treatment," which represents retaliation or punishment, purposefully being quiet together opens families up to a more spacious manner of being with each other. With eyes closed or softly open, be still without any words and, for a short time, share the silence.

The second Secret, **BE Present**, when exercised with an intimate partner, can result in meeting each other at surprising new depths. With no expectation, you enter into this exercise by breathing slowly and deliberately, until you feel you are truly sharing this moment, not racing ahead to the next.

BE Aware, the third Secret, is groundbreaking for couples who may realize that they have never looked at each other in this unfiltered way. The roles played in a family become formalized over time, and identities become fixed. People think they are looking, but do they really make it a point to gaze lovingly?

The fourth Secret, to **BE Attuned**, means to listen fully. Creating a process where everyone gets heard can trigger important changes, moving families toward healthier communication. Listening sessions, where each person is given time to speak without interruption, can be extremely beneficial. For those who are surrounding the speaker with pure listening, there should be no agenda. When you are close to someone, you can come to anticipate what they will say; but let yourself listen in a fresh way and be amazed by what you hear. *Listening to understand*, rather than speaking to explain, defend, or get approval, can become the new norm.

The fifth Secret, **BE Positive**, is based on genuine encouragement. Acknowledgments, congratulations, and other sincere words of praise are always gratifying. An expression of appreciation—not about how a person behaved but about who that person is in an essential way—can warm and heal the hearts of both giver and receiver. Young children, who are still learning about their natural capacities, are especially in need of such nourishment. Feeding our young with generous amounts of positive feedback enables them to thrive.

In the sixth Secret, **BE Connected**, partners can discover how to establish and enhance lines of communication. Long-lasting fulfillment happens when each person finds a path into the other's heart. Compassion is one way to transmit understanding and love. Many disagreements would be eased if people could simply have empathy for what another thinks and feels. Sex is more satisfying when we have developed a deeper connection of body, self, and soul with another. "Reaching a quiet ecstasy" is how one couple described it.

BE Yourself, the seventh Secret, is about being authentic. It is liberating to give voice to both your joy and your pain, and to be heard by those who love you. In a family where more value is placed on unique self-expression than on compliance, everyone feels free to expand and grow. Parents can model authentic speaking for children, guiding them to trust their true natures.

An adult child can heal old wounds and resentments by speaking words of love and forgiveness to aging parents. Tremendous relief also can be gained by sharing your memories of childhood without judgment or blame. Perhaps you will finally receive the kind of recognition from a parent that you have ached for all your life.

Deathbed communications are often the final opportunity for reconciliation between a child and parent. When a parent or child apologizes, finally speaks the words "I love you," or offers a long embrace, lifelong bitterness can be released. This can heal, in a single moment, a lifetime of disconnection or disempowerment.

Our social and family cultures would be different if we valued Essential Speaking. With more compassion and reciprocity, we increase our ability to face and creatively solve life's problems together.

> **Remember to apply the *7 Secrets to Essential Speaking* with family:**
>
> - **Be together in silence.**
> - **Share a moment of non-doing.**
> - **Gaze softly and lovingly.**
> - **Listen to understand.**
> - **Shower appreciations.**
> - **Find the path to the heart.**
> - **Value the unique.**

Essential Speaking at Work

Just as you can increase your ability to be connected and engaged with yourself and with friends and family, you can also practice the 7 Secrets at work to improve relationships and increase your effectiveness. If you are in a traditional business setting, you most likely are involved in conversations throughout the day. People who work together continually speak with one another to accomplish business tasks and reach shared goals. Even a sole proprietor with no staff must frequently interact with others.

To reach company goals, a business relies first and foremost on good communication. Business owners need to articulate their vision so that others feel motivated to produce and market the concept. Managers need to speak to groups and individuals in order to lead them. Workers must listen and pay attention to instructions so they can effectively perform their jobs, and often must ask questions to clarify instructions or provide input to their superiors to improve operations. Project teams gather to brainstorm ideas, and sales teams collaborate on how to present a product or service. A board of directors negotiates policy decisions and is often challenged by how to convey messages to stockholders. Everyone in a business plays an important role.

Speaking and listening among employers and employees is crucial, but communicating effectively with customers is even more important. Listening to them and understanding their motivation for buying are critical to your business success. Using language to influence them to spend their money on you rather than on a competitor is also crucial. Generating a satisfied user for life is the ultimate goal, and ongoing support and contact is the ideal means to maintaining a long-lasting, mutually beneficial relationship.

When examined from any angle, the gold in business is made and delivered through positive communications. Since the 7 Secrets have been shown to improve communication, it stands to reason that a business incorporating them will increase its profitability. Applications of the Steps can be made throughout the company, from the manufacturing line where workers do routine labor, to the showroom where buyers make their decisions.

The first Secret, **BE Silent**, if implemented creatively, could bring about a profound shift in a work environment. A manager who initiates a moment of silence prior to the start of staff meetings might be going against the corporate culture, but the risk could pay off. Instruct the group to take just one breath in order to prepare themselves to relax and get centered before you address what is on the agenda. A leader who takes the time to create a moment of empty space gives a message that there is value in the way people approach their undertakings. A person who is composed when discussing a project will likely have more impact, and members of a committee who are relaxed will be more open and receptive to what is being said and better able to express their own ideas.

The second Secret, **BE Present**, is particularly important when a service provider comes face-to-face with a client. A doctor who sits and relates to a patient in an unhurried fashion may be hard to fathom in this age of overcrowded health facilities. With people in the waiting room and only fifteen minutes allotted to each person, it is still imperative to concentrate on the medical problem without neglecting the human being beneath the stethoscope.

The third Secret, **BE Aware**, involves the skill of looking directly at the person with whom you are engaging. At restaurants, I notice and care if wait staff are paying attention to me. I feel more welcomed when there is a warm greeting in their eyes.

The fourth Secret, **BE Attuned**, is central to all business transactions. Listening is at the core, from sales to customer care. Being able to hear your customers' distinctive needs and satisfy them both before and after a buying decision increases your company's worth. Conflict resolution relies on being able to hear and respond to a problem without getting personally involved.

The fifth Secret, **BE Positive**, is a strategic approach that managers can use to motivate their employees and that employees can use as well. Rather than looking for what is wrong in a person's work, affirming the positive can boost morale and provide a great deal of incentive for improving performance. Framing feedback into productive suggestions to increase behaviors that are working will always be more fruitful than insults and threats.

The sixth Secret, **BE Connected**, will boost your ability to effectively relate to anyone in the work arena. This skill helps you engage in conversations about any subject matter with coworkers or managers. Every interaction, from a light and breezy chat at the coffee machine to a serious discussion about a raise, will go more smoothly when you are open and approachable.

The seventh Secret, **BE Yourself**, is at the foundation of our life's work. Knowing your purpose and conveying this in what you offer to the world is a reward you can enjoy every day. The ultimate expression of your passion, coupled with healthy remuneration, creates work that is sustaining. If you are still advancing toward greater clarification of your work mission, heed the signs pointing you toward activities and settings where you feel most completely yourself.

Whatever work you do, it can always be improved when there is good communication. Regardless of the level of your position, make it a point to interact in a positive manner with everyone in your business environment. Your words may seal a deal, but it is your presence that facilitates the connection that is shared.

Remember to apply the *7 Secrets to Essential Speaking* at work:

- **Start meetings with a moment of silence.**
- **Really be present with your clients.**
- **Look at your customers.**
- **Listen for how to satisfy distinctive needs.**
- **Motivate employees with affirmative feedback.**
- **Make yourself approachable.**
- **Know your purpose.**

Essential Speaking for World Peace

As a Peace Corps volunteer in the 1970s, I lived in Malaysia for two years, assigned to a residence surrounded by Indian, Chinese, and Malay neighbors. Every day, walking to and from the bus stop, I passed dwellings exploding with the pungent scents of Indian curry. As I walked further, I heard the clink of mah-jongg tiles punctuated by the laughter of Chinese elders as they played their favorite gambling game. The Indian homes with their strong aromas and the Chinese abodes with their clattering sounds were bordered by "kampongs" where indigenous Malay families squeezed into cramped wooden shacks. Enormous banana tree fronds served to umbrella these occupants from monsoon rains.

My Malaysian multicultural neighborhood was where the true work of peace-building occurred. The daily foreign exchanges took place in smiles, waves, and eventually, conversations. I made valuable practical contributions in my job as a vocational counselor, but the deep understanding that developed between this young woman from the United States and the families living near me fulfilled the original intent of that idealistic international volunteer program.

By the time I was serving in Southeast Asia, and long before I developed the Essential Speaking program presented in this book, I was already constructing symbolic bridges between people. I had come to know the power of connection and engagement from my hours of community service. The slogan of the 1960s, "If you're not part of the solution, you're part of the problem," inspired me through high school and college. Extracurricular activities took me into communities where I taught young Hispanic children, counseled unwed teenage mothers, and organized factory workers.

At an early age, my efforts toward social change brought me face to face with people of all nationalities and from all walks of life. Somehow I possessed a natural ability to put myself in someone else's shoes and relate to his or her point of view. If I disagreed, I could still take in and hear what was being said.

I used to judge myself as wishy-washy because, when I spoke, I rarely made opinionated declarations. Now, I value the mild nature of empathic listening and speaking from my heart. I consider these to be my core strengths and I employ them every day in my work as a psychologist. I also see these essential communication skills as the foundation stones of a productive peace program.

The *7 Secrets to Essential Speaking* have their roots in my dream of universal peace. As a child, I felt that opening my own mind and heart, and encouraging others to do the same, gave rise to compassion—one that could solve the conflicts I witnessed in family interactions, on city streets across the country, and between warring nations around the globe.

As an adult, I still believe that people being together, listening to each other, and speaking without fear significantly reduces misunderstandings and increases the bonds of human tenderness.

Each of the 7 Secrets represents a path to inner peace and peaceful co-existence among citizens throughout the world. If only one man makes a committed practice of expanding the silent reverie in his life, he may better withstand his personal ordeals. As a result, that man may be less reactive to chaotic situations and, in turn, be a source of solace to those around him.

Starting with Secret 1, we see the value of Essential Speaking in generating peacefulness in all realms of life. To **BE Silent** influences a profound inner tranquility that benefits personal health and well-being. When a large congregation gathers purposefully to share quiet time, the positive effects are multiplied. Group meditation, peace vigils, and praying with others all increase the feeling of a community working together for a unified cause. Anti-war demonstrations, protests against capital punishment, and boycotts targeting companies that pollute the environment are often delivered with shouts of rage. But when hundreds or thousands of people stand up, join hands, and remain completely still, their intentional silence causes a truly deafening reverberation.

BE Present is a path that many spiritual traditions throughout time have called an "entrance to the divine." Like the hidden door into a secret garden, you only have to know where it is in order to enter. The paradox is that there is nowhere to look but in the moment. A garden is a good analogy, since it is nature that teaches us about being in the here and now.

Sit back, lift your head, and find the clouds in the sky. Notice that they form and dissolve at the same time. Their impermanence is part of their beauty. What if we saw ourselves like the clouds, with each moment of our lives taking fantastic shape and then rapidly disintegrating? Might we have a different perspective on our own brief importance?

BE Aware is about looking at others. If we extend our vision into the heart and soul, we might see more commonalities than differences. If we only see the shape or color of another's eyes, we miss the vast inner dimensions, so similar to our own, that lie beyond. If we only notice the color of skin and reject our fellow beings on such superficial grounds, we diminish our own humanity.

BE Attuned gives those who oppose each other a new approach to mutual understanding. Listening that has a pure quality, like crystal spring water, is refreshing to people on both sides of an issue. In counseling couples, I train each partner to put a high priority on discovering what the other is trying to say. Rather than seek to explain himself, a husband is asked to seek more insight into his wife's side of the argument. This spirit of listening and allowing the full expression of another can be applied at the highest levels of peace negotiations.

BE Positive asserts that all children of the world are born with a sweet exuberance that endures forever. Cultural differences may diminish our awareness of this fact, but if we are conscious and teach ourselves how to affirm this basic vitality in everyone, we prevent the hate that arises out of ignorance. Rodgers and Hammerstein wrote a song for their Broadway musical, *South Pacific*, with these lyrics:

> *You've got to be taught before it's too late,*
> *before you are six or seven or eight,*
> *to hate all the people your relatives hate.*
> *You've got to be carefully taught!*

Children naturally grow into friendly and tolerant peacemakers if they aren't taught to hate by the adults in their lives.

If we are searching for more cohesive bonds with our neighbors who reside down the street and our sisters and brothers who inhabit all corners of the world, then the intention of friendship must be foremost in our hearts. Each one of us needs to refocus our view finders on the more buoyant qualities of others, learning how to identify and uphold the human Essence of beauty, strength, and radiance.

BE Connected is a reminder of a profound truth more than a new behavior to initiate. We see our individuality like a well that penetrates deep into the earth. At the bottom of each unique well is a common stream that feeds every living being. That stream is the life force. We are all one.

Wherever the circuitous route of our days may lead, and whatever the unique manner in which death calls to each of us, these unavoidable facts of life unite us as humans. All babies, whether they sleep in cribs draped with fine lace or in crates made of hard wooden slats, are totally dependent. Each one faces similar physical, mental, and emotional challenges in growing up. As toddlers we take our first steps, as young adults we make our mark, and as elders we either regret or embrace our legacy. The end of life, regardless of what one believes, entails a last breath before our bodies go cold. With these undeniable facts evident all around us, how can we deny our basic connection to every human being?

BE Yourself is an invitation to celebrate diversity. Dr. Martin Luther King Jr., who dreamed of justice and human rights for all humankind, laid down his life for this cause. Countless other noble men and women also have fought for dignity, equality, and self-expression.

Like explorers of a new world, we each go on a quest and seek the authentic Self. By crossing old boundaries and advancing into new inner terrains, we discover more of who we are. With this expansive sense of Self, genuine acceptance of all people can someday usher in an age of peace on earth.

Remember to apply the *7 Secrets to Essential Speaking* for World Peace:

- **Cultivate inner tranquility.**
- **Stand in the center of the now.**
- **Notice how similar we all are.**
- **Refresh yourself and others with pure, deep listening.**
- **Notice beauty, strength, and radiance in others.**
- **Join the flow that is the common stream of energy.**
- **Treasure yourself and celebrate diversity.**

Summary

There is a place for Essential Speaking whenever you communicate. Throughout your life—in your **own mind**, with your **family** and friends, at **work**, and even as you strive to bring about **world peace**—you can put your new skills to good use. Breaking free of the limitations that have inhibited your voice gives you greater power to express yourself throughout the day, in the most public of presentations and your most private conversations. At every moment, life extends an invitation to you to be fully yourself. Accept it, take the risk, and speak.

If you view each of the 7 Secrets as a journey toward greater enlightenment, then Essential Speaking will ultimately help you to tap into your own magnificence. This is the vision I hold as I coach an individual or lead a seminar. I am there to ease the fear of speaking in public, but also to encourage a fuller personal and even global transformation. I am working to transform the world from a collection of isolated, repressed, and highly competitive individuals into a richly textured, culturally diverse community of courageous people who speak and listen compassionately.

This is my path and my passion. May Essential Speaking help you discover your essential brilliance, embrace your life's purpose, and share your gifts fearlessly with the world.

Acknowledgments

I am grateful to my family and friends, my teachers, my coaching clients, and my workshop participants. I discovered the secrets to Finding Your Voice, but it was their involvement that helped me realize the power of presence and connection when it comes to speaking.

Ron Kane continually guided me to a deeper understanding of how to live each moment in full presence. Lee Glickstein, founder of Speaking Circles, provided the opening for me to overcome the fear of public speaking.

Naomi Rose listened to my words before they were even shaped and showed me how to write from my deeper Self. Joan Lester's positive response to my initial draft gave me strength to move forward in developing my ideas into chapters. Mindy Toomay's editing provided clarity and flow.

This book was gently ushered through all of its stages by Linda Joy Myers, my friend and an award-winning writer. The creative design and careful editing services were provided by Eaton Press.

To my partner, Earl Downing, I give special thanks for his ongoing support, uplifting spirit, and enduring embrace of the Secrets that are at the heart of *Essential Speaking*.

Index

A

anxiety about speaking, 14, 21, 17
attunement, 127
authentic
  Self, 9, 49, 63-64, 105, 109, 153
  speaking, 56, 144
awareness, 84, 152

B

BE Attuned, 15, 65, 83-88, 105, 125-128, 139, 143, 147, 151
BE Aware, 15, 65, 76-82, 105, 123-125, 138, 143, 147, 151
BE Connected, 15, 65, 95, 99, 106, 130-132, 139, 144, 147, 152
BE Positive, 15, 65, 89-95, 106, 128-130, 139, 143, 147, 152
BE Present, 15, 65, 71-76, 105, 120-122, 138, 143, 147, 151
BE Silent, 15, 65, 66-71, 105, 118-120, 138, 142, 146, 150
BE Yourself, 15, 65, 66, 99-106, 132-133, 139, 144, 148, 153

C

confidence, 11, 13, 20, 25, 39, 40, 47, 53-60, 62-66, 72-74, 84, 103, 122, 132-133, 137
connect
  with yourself, 67
  with one person at a time, 135

E

essential
  Being, 62, 64
  listening, 84
  Self, 24, 51, 55, 58, 61, 64, 77, 109, 126, 138-141
  Speaking Practice Group, 25, 112-115, 135

F

find your voice, 24, 109, 112
fear
  of being your true self, 49
  of speaking, 12, 25, 27, 29, 31, 35, 39, 47, 59, 60, 65, 85, 110, 136, 154

G

Glickstein, Lee, 21, 23, 72, 85, 95, 111

K

Kane, Ron, 52, 155

L

Listening, 117, 126-127, 131, 134, 136, 139, 143, 146-147
looking
  deeply, 130
  directly at, 79, 105, 147
  into a pair of eyes, 124
  for the best, 95
  for their beauty, 93
  for your faults, 129

M

Mastering the 7 Secrets to Essential Speaking, 107-114

O

overcome
  anxiety, 17, 52
  fear, 21, 47, 51, 60, 65, 112, 136
  stage fright, 11, 22-23

P

power of your presence, 111, 118
practicing
  each secret, 118, 136
  in a group, 24, 112
  on your own, 24, 111
programs with Doreen Downing, PhD, 163

R

Ram Dass, 69
Real
  fear, 52, 59
  Self, 49, 58, 60, 65, 94, 112, 134

S

Self
authentic, 9, 49, 63-64, 105, 109, 153
essential, 24, 51, 55, 58, 61, 64, 77, 109, 126, 138, 139, 140, 141
real, 49, 58, 60, 65, 94, 112, 134
true, 49, 57, 102, 103
Speaking Circles, 21-24, 52, 55, 56, 90, 95, 111, 163

Speaking
 in front of groups, 14, 17
 in public, 12, 27, 29, 31, 35, 43, 47, 68, 102, 104, 137, 154
 stage fright 11, 22, 23, 29, 31, 32, 35, 37, 40, 43, 58, 96, 112

T

Toastmasters, 20, 52, 53
transformation, 11, 58, 77, 109, 113, 154
true Self, 49, 57, 102, 103

W

Wohlman, Gary, 21, 47

About the Author

Earlier in my career as a clinical psychologist, as I was helping others overcome their fears, I carried a hidden terror of my own. I was afraid to speak in public.

I have discovered that the key to confident speaking is being fully present and connected to my essential Self.

After earning a degree in sociology in the 1960s, my life path led to Malaysia as a Peace Corps volunteer. I realized that at the core of social problems were communication and relationship issues. I returned to get a PhD in counseling psychology from the University of California, Berkeley and began my private practice in the 1980s.

I believe my calling is to facilitate personal and professional transformation and to help people recover their vibrant inner spirit and speak without fear.

I now teach others how to dissolve stage fright forever through Private Coaching, Speaking Circles, Fearless Speaking Workshops, and Self-Guided E-Courses. I also co-lead the Speaking Circle Facilitator Certification Program and have trained facilitators who now practice in Canada, Europe, India, and Asia.

Where to Find Programs with Doreen Downing, PhD

As a licensed clinical psychologist, Doreen specializes in the treatment of anxiety related to the fear of public speaking. Individual and group coaching sessions are offered in person in Berkeley, California, or virtually on Zoom. Authentic Speaking Seminars are conducted worldwide. You can find out more about her offerings by going to her website, https://essentialspeaking.com/.

As a podcast host of *Find Your Voice, Change Your Life*, Doreen interviews people who once felt like they did not have a voice. She invites them to share how they found their voice and what they offer now that they have the confidence to be more fully expressed. See: https://findyourvoicechangeyourlife.com/.

As training director of Speaking Circles International, Doreen conducts Speaking Circle Facilitator Trainings where you can be certified to lead professional groups on how to be present, connected, and authentic when you speak. See: https://speakingcirclesinternational.com/.

She has led week-long transformational retreats in Hawaii, "SpeakingQuest: Journey to your Authentic Self." See: https://speakingquest.com/.

You can connect with Doreen and her work through any of the following channels:

WEBSITES

Main website: https://essentialspeaking.com

Course website: https://essential-speaking.thinkific.com

Training Director, Speaking Circles International: https://speakingcirclesinternational.com/about-us/

Relational Presence: https://relationalpresence.com

SOCIAL MEDIA

LinkedIn: https://linkedin.com/in/drdoreenh/

Facebook Profile: https://facebook.com/drdoreendowning/

Facebook Business Page: https://facebook.com/EssentialSpeaking

Facebook Book Page: https://facebook.com/essentialspeakingbook

Instagram: https://instagram.com/essentialspeaking/

Twitter: https://twitter.com/drdoreenh

Pinterest: https://pinterest.com/essentialspeaking

YouTube Channel: https://youtube.com/user/drdoreenh

PODCASTS

Podcast Playlist: https://findyourvoicechangeyourlife.com

www.ingramcontent.com/pod-product-compliance
Lightning Source LLC
Chambersburg PA
CBHW050234120526
44590CB00016B/2083